Mom, Are You There?

FINDING A PATH TO PEACE
THROUGH ALZHEIMER'S

KATHLEEN A. NEGRI

forget-me-not press

This is a work of nonfiction.

Book design by Boulder Bookworks
Inside photo collage of Patricia Negri by Jennifer White
Inside photo of Patricia Negri seated in chair, © 2003 Susann J. Gordon

For information, please contact:
forget-me-not press
P.O. Box 587, Wheat Ridge, Colorado, 80034
www@SteppingStonesToPeace.com

ISBN 0-9763557-0-1

Library of Congress Catalog Card Number 2005901047

Printed in the United States of America

FOR

PATRICIA

❀

If he had learned
something profound in his life,
it was this:

That to ask a question
could be the most rebellious of acts
and the most necessary.

That allowing words to go unspoken
could cause not only harm to oneself
but harm to another.

MARY RELINDES ELLIS,
The Turtle Warrior

❀

CONTENTS

❀

	Preface	ix
ONE	A Question of Peace	1
TWO	The First Step in the Journey	9
THREE	Who Can I Turn to for Information and Support?	21
FOUR	Obtain a Diagnosis	27
FIVE	Complete Legal and Financial Planning	37
SIX	Build a Safety Net	57
SEVEN	How Do I Prepare Myself for this Journey?	69
EIGHT	How Can I Stay Open to the Gifts this Experience has to Offer?	85
NINE	Leave Your Own Agenda at Home	93
TEN	Let Go of the Past	101
ELEVEN	Reveal Your True Self	111
TWELVE	Pay Attention to Your Loved One as if She is a Prophet	119
THIRTEEN	Express and Record Your Travels	127
FOURTEEN	One Last Story – Pulling it all Together	133
FIFTEEN	Mom, Are You There?	143
EPILOGUE	Eulogy for a Mother	151
	Endnotes	155
	Additional Resources	157
	Recommendations for Further Reading	163
	Index	167
	Order Form	172

ACKNOWLEDGMENTS

❀

For showing me the path, Pamela J. Gordon, Carole Jacobs, Sally Kurtzman, Rosa Mazone, and Jennifer White

To the early readers for their invaluable feedback, Beth Fox, Kathleen Lantz, and Susan Stern

For technical assistance, Beth Fox, Susan Hellman, Jytte Lokvig, Marilyn Mitchell, Donald J. Murphy, M.D., John D. Peterson, Marcia Reish, and Jacqueline M. Roth

PREFACE

❀

This is a love story. Not in the traditional sense, but in all the ways that describe how unconditional love can bring two lives together, opening the door to understanding and forgiveness.

It is the story of my mother, Patricia, and her struggle with Alzheimer's. But, ultimately, it is my story, too. It is my account of how my mother's illness challenged and inspired me to look differently at Alzheimer's and myself. To recognize that accompanying a loved one on the journey through dementia can be a powerful catalyst for personal growth and transformation, one that can bring untold gifts into your life—as it did into mine.

Much has been written about the devastation wrought by dementia and of its ability to tear families apart. Little is written of its power to also bring them together. By sharing with you the many ways in which my mother's dementia *enriched* my life and my relationships, it is my fervent hope to offer you a different perspective—one that is both positive and life affirming—so that you may also willingly accept this journey into your life.

My father was my mother's 24-hour caregiver; my time with her provided a brief respite from his daily care. Still, by fully embracing my mother's diagnosis and by actively participating in her care as she declined, I embarked on an unexpected and amazing journey that has led me to better understanding myself: Who I am, why I think and feel as I do, and how I take responsibility for my life.

In the process, I learned to let go of all the ways I had previously defined my mother, heal many of the childhood wounds I had attributed to her, and thus transform the long-strained relationship I had with her. In setting my mother free from my clouded vision of her, I freed myself as well—from my *childhood box* full of distrust, hurt and anger that had kept me from living my life more fully. Out of this healing and understanding, I came to a place of peace and acceptance of my mother—and of myself.

As I walked beside my mother during the last three years of her life on a path full of sharp turns, hidden hazards, and unforgiving precipices, I uncovered several simple strategies—*stepping stones*—that helped me gain firmer footing on our journey through Alzheimer's. What follows is a road map to those strategies that can help you find your path to peace as you care for a parent, family member or friend with this devastating illness.

I realize your situation may be very different from mine. You may have enjoyed a healthy and loving relationship with your loved one, only to have it "destroyed" by dementia. For you, it may be difficult to see how Alzheimer's can enrich your life. While I support you in this place, it is my hope that this book will speak to you nonetheless by suggesting ways to recapture or redefine what you feel you have lost in this relationship.

I write both as an Elder Law attorney and as someone who is a caregiver and daughter. My goal is to offer both practical tips to help you plan ahead for the medical, legal and financial issues raised by long-term illness and death, along with personal stories. These stories illuminate the many gifts I received from my mother and illustrate the personal growth I experienced on this journey with her. Each gift, each transformation, became the mortar that connected the stepping stones on my path to peace through Alzheimer's. Perhaps these stories will trigger memories for you and help you to fully realize these benefits for yourself.

Each Chapter ends with a few suggestions for you to consider when expressing and recording your travels with your loved one and some practical questions to get you thinking about what actions need to be taken. These exercises are intended to:

1. Challenge you to *think* differently about yourself and your relationships so that you can begin to identify the hidden gifts and the ways in which dementia can positively transform your life; and

2. Help you to *strategize* and prepare for the practicalities of this journey. This way, you can immediately begin to pave your own path to peace through Alzheimer's.

At the end, you will find a section of "Additional Resources." This contains contact information for the organizations and individuals mentioned in this book, national caregiver resources, and some suggestions for additional reading to support and guide you on your journey.

Traveling with a loved one through Alzheimer's *can* be a gift in your life—if you choose to see it this way. In this book I share with you how, by asking the right questions of yourself and others, you can thrive despite the overwhelming obstacles presented by a devastating illness such as Alzheimer's.

I hope to encourage you to embrace your loved one's illness, whatever the situation may be, so that you may find your own path to peace—one that is strong and firmly cemented with the many gifts and transformations you may discover as you accompany your loved one on this final journey.

ONE

A Question of Peace

Hope is an orientation of the spirit, an orientation of the heart. It is not the conviction that something will turn out well, but the certainty that something makes sense, regardless of how it turns out.

VACLAV HAVEL

✤

"I'm happy to see you."

This was the third time my mother had made that comment in five minutes. She was typically polite, even pleasant. But the truth was I wasn't sure she knew who I was—at least not at that moment. And so I sat at the kitchen table, next to my mother, and wondered: Mom, are you there?

Like millions of Americans today, my mother lived in a fractured world of dementia; a solitary place of loss and confinement.

What we know of this disease is terrifying. Alzheimer's is a progressive, incurable disease that robs the brain first of memory, language and reasoning before it shuts down the most basic of bodily functions. What we don't yet understand is what it is like to *be* the person with Alzheimer's. No one has returned from this devastating illness to tell his story.

Later that morning, my mother and I were out walking the dog on a fall day, the air crisp and clean.

"It's beautiful out, isn't it, Kathleen?"

Suddenly, the door to my mother's mind opened a crack and we connected. I hugged her and, for a brief time, my mother was mine again. Even now, after my mother's death in July 2004, I hold tight to that feeling, cherishing it for the gold that it is. And I am reminded that there is still much to learn from my mother and from Alzheimer's.

The notion that people with Alzheimer's have something to teach us may seem odd to you. After all, we are taught to think of Alzheimer's purely in terms of its losses. But there are lessons in Alzheimer's nonetheless, and I set out to find them ... by doing what my training as an attorney had taught me to do. I learned to ask the right questions at the right time—and to listen carefully for the answers.

A SEARCH FOR MEANING

As an Elder Law attorney, questions are one of the most powerful tools I have to help my clients and their families find answers to the issues raised by long-term illness and death. In this role, I've become an expert at asking:

"How much money do you have?"

"Have you looked at nursing homes yet?"

"What about divorcing your spouse?"

I recognize that these questions are intrusive, heartbreaking, and often life changing. But even with all of my experience, never once did I imagine that my family and I would be the ones *answering* those questions … that like the 19 million families impacted by this disease, we would be looking for clarity and understanding on behalf of a loved one with Alzheimer's.

Up until the day of my mother's diagnosis, I thought I *knew* all the questions. After all, I had been successfully practicing Elder Law for more than a decade. I also thought I *had* all the answers. But there I sat, watching as Alzheimer's unraveled my mother's life—and mine.

So what is it about questions that make us so uncomfortable? Why is it so difficult to ask them—and why is it even harder to hear the answers?

From childhood, we're taught that we ask questions to get information.

"What is Alzheimer's?"

"It is an incurable, fatal disease that causes the loss of brain function."

But questions aren't always that straightforward. They can take us to an unknown, unsettling destination.

"How long can my mother live with this disease?"

"It's hard to say. Five years. Ten years. I've seen some patients live twenty years with Alzheimer's."

We think of questions as being factual. Black or white. Right or wrong. But sometimes, they can be a plea for forgiveness.

"Doctor, if we had brought Mom in sooner, would the prognosis have been different?"

"We can't know for sure."

If questions are so tricky, why ask them? Questions are crucial if you want to get through a devastating illness, such as Alzheimer's, and come out whole on the other side. The right questions tell you what you need to know about dementia. They can help you cut through the chaos. They can help you find peace.

One fact stands out above all others. It is that men and women who have dementia have emerged from the places where they were hidden away; they have walked onto the stage of history, and begun to be regarded as persons in the full sense. Dementia, as a concept, is losing its terrifying associations with the raving lunatic in the old-time asylum. It is being perceived as an understandable and human condition, and those who are affected by it have begun to be recognized, welcomed, embraced and heard. The achievements of biomedical science, although so much vaunted in the media, are insignificant in comparison to this quiet revolution.

TOM KITWOOD,
Dementia Reconsidered: the person comes first [1]

THE JOURNEY BEGINS

In 2001, when my mother's physician confirmed my family's worst fears that my mother had Alzheimer's disease, I asked myself the first of many questions: How was I going to get through this? As I considered the possibilities, I recognized I had a choice to make. I could let fear and anger define the time we had left together. Or, I could choose another path.

I chose a path to peace through Alzheimer's; a path that began when I asked myself the following three questions:

1. **Who can I turn to for information and support?**

2. **How do I prepare myself for this journey?**

3. **How can I stay open to the gifts this experience has to offer?**

These questions became my stepping stones as they guided me on my journey with my mother. They helped me to navigate the many changes to my mother's life and mine that resulted from this disease.

For my mother, this change came unwillingly, and perhaps unknowingly, because she had no choice in the matter of her having dementia. But for me, Alzheimer's was a positive catalyst for change in my life precisely because I chose to *embrace* my mother's dementia, to become actively involved in her life, and to relate to her in a new way. The key was asking the right questions to help me uncover the possibilities. As simplistic as this may sound, the same can work for you.

In essence, dementia stripped away many of the negative elements of my mother's personality—the hard-wiring that had previously blocked our ability to connect. She was no longer the cold, distant, critical parent of my youth; she had become more loving and expressive. It was as if Alzheimer's had given my mother permission, along with a new set of skills, to be a different person in how she related to the people around her.

The bottom line is that dementia offered us a way out of the old patterns and behaviors that had kept us boxed up and separated. As I asked questions about my mother's disease and of myself, I learned a new way of relating. My mother and I unexpectedly came together on this common ground called dementia and it made all the difference, in both of our lives.

It all started with these three simple questions. I believe these same questions can change your experience with Alzheimer's. I know this because they changed mine.

Suggestions for Expressing and Recording Your Travels:

Is it difficult for you to ask questions? What kinds of questions are difficult? Why?

_____

_____

_____

_____

_____

How do you relate to your loved one's disease? Do you find yourself fighting the situation, or like me, can you find ways to embrace it? Why or why not?

_____

_____

_____

_____

_____

Make a list of the emotions you feel about the words "dementia" and "Alzheimer's." Then think about each emotion and unmask its impact. Could it be that your anger is really fear? Is your impatience really confusion?

_____

_____

_____

_____

_____

Practical Suggestions to Help You Pave Your Path:

Consider the strengths you bring to this journey; then consider your weaknesses. As a caregiver, what steps can you take to lead with your strengths and minimize your frustrations?

Make a list of your goals as a caregiver. Include your personal goals and those for your loved one.

Look at your own health issues and schedule an appointment with your doctor to discuss any concerns you have about your health or your ability to care for your loved one.

The First Step in the Journey

*A journey of a thousand miles begins
with a single step.*

L A O - T Z U

❀

My mother was a vigorous, energetic woman—the model house-wife. That is, until one day when, without warning, she stopped cooking. She stopped cleaning. She stopped doing laundry. She just sat down and stopped.

I knew something was wrong. But no one in my family seemed to question her behavior. Perhaps they thought my mother's memory lapses were perfectly normal for a 65 year-old woman. Her inability to name common objects was just part of her "quirky" personality. Her sudden loss of vanity was just a "passing phase." And so for five unsettling years, Alzheimer's moved in—becoming the uninvited, unquestioned, and unwelcome guest in our household.

Why did my family wait so long to get help? And how did we let Alzheimer's become the "two-ton elephant" sitting in the middle of our living room?

Like many families impacted by this devastating and often-times confusing disease, we hid behind a wall of denial and anger.

WHAT IS ALZHEIMER'S DISEASE?

Alzheimer's (AHLZ-high-merz) disease is a progressive, degen-erative disease that destroys cells in the brain. First described by the German neurologist Alois Alzheimer, this most common form of dementia is characterized by impaired memory, thinking and behavior.

Research has found that the brains of Alzheimer's patients show a build-up of insoluble protein deposits in the spaces between nerve cells (called plaques) and within the nerve cells themselves (called tangles). What triggers this build-up of protein in the brain is still a mystery. However, abnormal changes to these nerve structures cause the communications pathways to break down and become permanently disconnected. When messages are no longer able to be transmitted, certain aspects of brain function may be lost.[2]

THE SILENT BEGINNING

In most people, Alzheimer's gains a foothold quietly—at least at first. In fact, experts believe that Alzheimer's begins to make changes in the brain as many as 10 to 20 years before any visible symptoms of the disease appear. Not surprisingly, early evidence of the disease, such as memory loss and mood shifts, is often mis-taken for the effects of normal aging.

In reality, these changes are anything but normal. Alzheimer's typically follows a pattern of deterioration that is often broken down into three major stages, commonly referred to as Early, Middle and Late, or Mild, Moderate and Severe. Understanding these stages provides a reference point—a road map—for understanding the progression of the disease. The Alzheimer's Association provides the following description of the three stages of Alzheimer's:[3]

STAGE 1: EARLY [MILD]

- Loss of memory about recent occasions or events
- Word or name-finding problems and loss of train of thought
- Noticeable performance issues in social or work settings
- Loses or misplaces familiar objects
- Increased difficulty with planning and organization
- Decreased capacity to perform complex tasks such as planning dinner or managing finances
- Loses spark or zest for life—does not start anything
- Loses judgment about money
- Has difficulty with new learning
- Has trouble finding words—may substitute or make up words that sound like or mean something like the forgotten word
- Has trouble organizing or thinking logically
- Asks repetitive questions
- Withdraws, loses interest, is irritable, not as sensitive to others' feelings, uncharacteristically angry when frustrated or tired

- Won't make decisions—for example, when asked what she wants to eat, says "I'll have what she is having"
- Takes longer to do routine chores and becomes upset if rushed or if something unexpected happens
- Constantly checks, searches or hoards things of no value

STAGE 2: MIDDLE [MODERATE]

- Disorientation to time, date and season
- Difficulty with numbers, balancing checkbook and mathematical challenges
- Difficult with sequencing tasks such as bathing, driving, eating or dressing
- Mood and personality changes may begin to occur
- May experience sleep or appetite disturbances
- Memories may be selective or relative to early life experiences
- Increased incontinence of bladder or bowel
- May become restless, wander or pace
- May develop repetitive speech or behavior patterns
- Changes in behavior, concern for appearance, hygiene, and sleep become more noticeable
- Mixes up identity of people, such as thinking a son is a brother or that a wife is a stranger
- Poor judgment or reasoning ability creates safety issues when left alone
- Cannot organize thoughts or follow logical explanations; has trouble following written notes or

completing tasks; makes up stories to fill in gaps in memory

- May accuse, threaten, curse, fidget or behave inappropriately, such as kicking, hitting, biting, screaming or grabbing
- May see, hear, smell or taste things that are not there

STAGE 3: LATE [SEVERE]

- Lost awareness of recent experiences and events and of surroundings
- May recognize family as family but is unable to use names or endearment
- Becomes dependent on others to manage daily care
- May become completely incontinent
- Unable to walk, show appropriate affection or hold head up
- Swallowing and eating difficulties
- Muscles grow rigid and reflexes become abnormal
- Lost weight and skin elasticity causing skin to tear easily
- May develop repetitive behaviors or sounds
- Doesn't recognize self or close family
- Speaks in gibberish, is mute, or is difficult to understand
- May repetitively cry out, pat or touch everything
- May have seizures, frequent infections, falls
- Forgets how to walk or is too unsteady or weak to stand alone
- Sleeps more

THE EARLIER, THE BETTER

Because the earliest symptoms of Alzheimer's are often hard to discern by most, except trained professionals, many patients aren't diagnosed until they are in the second stage of the disease. Yet when it comes to getting the help you and your loved one need, early intervention is crucial. That's because, as Alzheimer's progresses, the doors to many medical, legal and financial options slam shut.

Doors of opportunity, such as:

- Drug therapies that can slow the progression of Alzheimer's … but only if started in the early stage of the disease.

- Planning options that can help preserve a person's independence and protect assets … but only while the client has the ability to take part in the decision making.

- Health care options that allow a person to remain at home for as long as possible … but only when community resources are put in place early on.

When it came to getting my mother help, the battle lines were drawn early in my family. On the one side, I was fighting to get my mother the medical attention that I was convinced she needed. On the other side, my father and siblings appeared unprepared to accept, at this time, that Mom was desperately ill. Complicating the issue was my parents' long-held distrust of the medical profession and my father's fear of my mother's temper, which seemed to flare at the slightest provocation.

"I have to live with her, Kathleen. Stop nagging me about getting her in to see a doctor. Besides, if it's Alzheimer's, there's nothing he can do for your mother anyway."

Like many adult children watching a parent decline, it's difficult to know when and how hard to push. In the case of our mother, it took more than five years before my sister and I were finally able to get her to see a doctor. And even then, it wasn't easy.

"*Let it go, Kathleen. There's nothing wrong with me.*"

Round and round we went, my mother and me arguing in the kitchen. Exasperated finally, I issued an ultimatum:

"*Mom, you have a choice. Either you can go voluntarily to see Dr. Murphy on Thursday afternoon, or I will get a Court order forcing you to go. You choose.*"

"*You can't do that to me, Kathleen.*"

"*Of course I can. What do you think I do every day of the week in my job? I don't want to force you, Mom—I would rather you make the choice to voluntarily see the doctor.*"

My mother's eyes narrowed as she leaned in, close to my face, angry.

"*You wouldn't do that to me.*"

The moment had come. I stood firm, holding her gaze.

"*Yes, I would. This has gone on long enough. You need to see a doctor and get some help, Mom.*"

"*I'll do whatever my husband tells me to do.*"

My husband? She was talking about my father as if I was a stranger. My mother appeared desperate, angry and scared—a powerful combination of emotions that made this intervention even more difficult. Despite the wall my mother was trying feverishly to put up, I saw an opening and decided to take it: I went outside to get my father.

I found him in his garden, bent over, with his face buried in foot-tall parsley—the perfect metaphor for how my Dad had handled the situation up until then. He knew what was going on inside the house and he wanted no part of it. Still, he reluctantly followed me inside.

"Mom and I were talking. I think it's time she saw a doctor. What do you think, Dad?"

My father stared down at his feet:

"Well, yes, Patty, I think you should see a doctor."

And with that, he turned to head back out to his garden—his safe haven, where everything was green and growing, still full of life; the place where it was easy to find solace among his beloved vegetables. Meanwhile, my mother had been backed into a corner.

"Fine. I'll go."

Later that week, as I drove my parents to the doctor's office, my mother grew more agitated and angry with each passing mile, obviously scared and distraught. Seated next to me in the front passenger seat, she was taking long, deep sighs and wringing her hands. Perhaps she understood, on some level, that her declining condition was about to be exposed to everyone. I locked the doors of the car just in case she changed her mind.

Now I Understand

Thinking back, I recognize now that this trip to the doctor's office was the first step in finding a path to peace through Alzheimer's. That's because obtaining a diagnosis helped us to understand what was happening to my mother and to begin processing our emotional responses to her dementia.

The diagnosis helped my father to shift his thinking. He finally saw that my mother wasn't being stubborn about not wanting to carry out simple tasks, such as brushing her teeth: She was sick. She no longer knew what to do with the toothbrush sitting in the glass by the bathroom sink. The memory of that routine activity was lost in a storm of neurological changes moving through her brain. The diagnosis of Alzheimer's gave my father a reference point. And with that, he began to help her willingly with many of her daily routines and to finally accept the help offered by his children and by outside health-care agencies.

The diagnosis also helped my siblings adjust their expectations of my mother and to choose for themselves what this journey would be like for them. In many instances, the four of us were finally able to work together for the benefit of our parents.

I do not think any of us would have come to this place of acceptance without an official diagnosis of Alzheimer's-type dementia (more about this in the next Chapter). The diagnosis wasn't the beginning of my mother's decline—that had started five years earlier when my mother first started exhibiting symptoms of dementia. The diagnosis was, instead, the beginning of our journey as a family, helping my mother to find her way through this devastating illness.

As I thought about the future and the inevitable course of my mother's disease, I realized I needed a plan to give my mother the care she needed and deserved. I asked myself: *"Who can I turn to for information and support?"* This simple question—and the answer it led to—was the first stepping stone on my path to peace through Alzheimer's.

Suggestions for Expressing and Recording Your Travels:

What are some of the barriers in your family to obtaining a diagnosis of Alzheimer's? As you think about them, what can you do to handle this process differently?

_____

_____

_____

_____

_____

Denial is a powerful emotion that can keep you from moving forward in your journey. How has denial factored into your family dynamics? What steps can you take to become more accepting of your loved one's disease?

_____

_____

_____

_____

_____

What are some of the symptoms of your loved one's illness? Can you identify what stage of Alzheimer's your loved one might be experiencing? How can you help your loved one compensate for his losses?

_____

_____

_____

_____

_____

Practical Suggestions to Help You Pave Your Path:

Compile the names of any friends and acquaintances who also have dealt with Alzheimer's disease. Contact them for referrals and information on how to get started with a diagnosis.

Keep a journal of the changes you see in your loved one and take it with you to your meeting with the doctor. This way, you will be able to help the doctor understand the chronology of what is happening to your loved one.

As you prepare for the visit to the doctor, you can smooth the path for your loved one by telling him that you have an appointment, redirect any objections and give him adequate time to get ready. You can also allay some of your loved one's anxiety and avoid a long wait at the doctor's office by calling ahead to check if the doctor is on time with appointments.

THREE

Who Can I Turn to for Information and Support?

We don't accomplish anything in this world alone ... and whatever happens is the result of the whole tapestry of one's life and all the weavings of individual threads from one to another that creates something.

SANDRA DAY O'CONNOR
Supreme Court Justice

❀

The Alzheimer's caregiver is often called the hidden or second victim of the disease. To strengthen and sustain yourself through this difficult journey you need all the support you can find. What kind of support?

- First, you need a doctor—one who specializes in dealing with the health issues of aging.

- Second, you need a lawyer—one who specializes in dealing with the legal and financial issues of aging.

- And, third, you need a support group—one that specializes in dealing with the issues of aging and dementia.

Why do you need these particular specialists? Isn't your family doctor enough? The answer is a resounding no.

Alzheimer's is the most common cause of dementia, but it isn't the only one. Depression, stroke, alcohol abuse, and even nutritional and vitamin deficiencies also can create memory loss and confusion. Only a geriatrician—a physician who specializes in age-related diseases—has the expertise necessary to pinpoint a diagnosis. If the diagnosis is Alzheimer's, a geriatrician can:

- Prescribe the latest drugs to slow it down;

- Counsel you on strategies to keep your loved one safe; and

- Help you understand the behavior and personality changes that may lie ahead.

CAUSES OF DEMENTIA[4]

56%	Alzheimer's Disease
4%	Brain Injury
14%	Vascular Causes or Multi-Infarct Dementia
12%	Multiple Causes
8%	Parkinson's Disease
6%	Other Causes

What about legal and financial planning? Isn't your family lawyer enough? The answer here is, also, no.

According to the Alzheimer's Association, the current average lifetime cost of Alzheimer's care is close to $175,000. That's enough to threaten the financial security of most families. Only an Elder Law attorney has both the legal and financial expertise to help you plan ahead for this expense. An Elder Law attorney can:

- Make sure the right legal documents are in place;
- Counsel you on Medicare and Medicaid options; and
- Help you preserve assets.

What about the emotional toll of Alzheimer's? You may be thinking: I have friends—aren't they enough? Again, the answer is no. Your friends may be the most loving in the world. But unless they have traveled through Alzheimer's, they won't have the roadmap—the skills—to guide you through this emotionally draining disease.

Groups, such as the Alzheimer's Association, can offer you access to:

- Training programs to help you care for your loved one;
- Support groups to help you cope with feelings of frustration, anxiety and depression; and
- Outreach services to help you leverage resources available right in your own community.

Medical specialists. Legal specialists. Support groups. The first step in finding your path to peace is to ask yourself: *"Who can I turn to for information and support?"* Then, surround yourself with people who can help:

- Specialists who understand long-term, catastrophic illness.

- Partners who can help you be the best caregiver possible.

- Companions who can provide the emotional support you need for yourself.

The following Chapters will guide you through strategies to connect with, and make the most of, these essential members of your team as you journey through Alzheimer's.

DID YOU KNOW?

- 7 out of 10 family caregivers are women.

- 19% of caregivers provide at least 40 hours of care per week (called "constant care").

- 31% of family caregivers who provide constant care report physical or mental health problems of their own.[5]

Suggestions for Expressing and Recording Your Travels:

Many caregivers believe they have to do it all. How willing are you to get the help you need? If the idea of consulting with doctors, lawyers, or social workers is uncomfortable for you, consider the reasons. Then, think about how you can begin to develop a network of professionals who can help you be the most effective caregiver you can be.

_____

_____

_____

_____

_____

Is your loved one the type of person who feels he can do it alone? That no help is needed? How can you facilitate connecting your loved one with the experts he will need to make it through this illness?

_____

_____

_____

_____

_____

Getting help may require that you reveal family secrets and deeply harbored resentments or issues regarding your loved one. How will you handle this should it happen? What can you do now to prepare yourself to handle the sensitive inquiries that may lie ahead?

_____

_____

_____

_____

_____

Practical Suggestions to Help You Pave Your Path:

Contact your local Chapter of the Alzheimer's Association and ask for referral lists to doctors and lawyers in your area who can assist you. Sign up for their free monthly newsletter, and also ask for a calendar of support groups and classes. To find the Chapter nearest to you, visit www.alz.org and type in your zip code.

Talk to friends and colleagues about their experiences dealing with doctors and lawyers as they navigated a devastating illness. What are their recommendations? What mistakes did they make that you can avoid?

Be sure to ask your doctor to rule out other diseases that act like Alzheimer's, including Vascular or Multi-Infarct dementia, Huntington's disease, dementia with Lewy Bodies, Parkinson's disease, Normal Pressure Hydrocephalus (NPH), Frontotemporal dementia (Pick's disease), and Kruetzfeldt-Jacob disease (CJD).

FOUR

Obtain a Diagnosis

*The world is round and the place
which may seem like the end may also
be only the beginning.*

IVY BAKER

❀

"*Yellow. Oldsmobile. Cabbage. Mrs. Negri, can you repeat these words?*"

When my mother couldn't respond to that question, I knew that our lives had changed forever. Three simple words and yet my mother couldn't repeat a single one:

"*Yellow. Oldsmobile. Cabbage.*"

The geriatrician we choose to evaluate my mother was Dr. Donald Murphy, a colleague with whom I had served on several volunteer committees on aging. While I was lucky to have this connection, it isn't difficult to locate a geriatrician who can give your loved one the care she needs. See the "Practical Suggestions" at the end of this Chapter.

We met in an examination room the size of a large walk-in closet—my parents, sister, the doctor and me, crammed together like shipwrecked passengers in a life raft, hanging on in shifting seas. Dr. Murphy began the consultation with a review of my mother's general medical and family history. He asked about the onset of her symptoms. He conducted a brief medical examination. And then, he concluded his clinical evaluation by administering the Folstein Mini Mental State Examination (MMSE).[6]

The MMSE is one of the most frequently used tools to diagnose dementia. The scoring of the MMSE ranges from 0 to 30 points, with:

- a score of 20 to 24 points suggesting mild impairment,
- a score of 16 to 19 points suggesting moderate impairment,
- a score of 10 to 15 points indicating moderately severe impairment, and
- a score of less than 10 points indicating severe impairment.

The MMSE consists of several sections, each measuring how a different part of the brain works by evaluating orientation to self, place, and time; memory and recall; attention and calculation; and language skills. The MMSE can be supplemented with additional testing for abstraction, problem solving, memory and insight, planning for emergency situations, etc., as the doctor deems necessary. The test is simple in format:

SECTION 1: ORIENTATION measures a patient's ability to answer correctly the following types of questions:
- What day is it?
- What is the name of your street?
- What building are we in?
- What year was last year?

SECTION 2: MEMORY (PART 1) tests a patient's ability to immediately repeat three words, such as: Yellow. Oldsmobile. Cabbage.

SECTION 3: ATTENTION AND CALCULATION assesses a patient's concentration by asking the person to complete a complex task, such as counting backwards from 50 by 5's.

SECTION 4: MEMORY (PART 2) tests whether the patient can recall the three words from Section 2.

SECTION 5: LANGUAGE SKILLS evaluates a patient's language, writing and drawing skills in six separate tasks. For example, the patient is asked to:

1. Name two everyday objects shown, such as a pencil and book.
2. Say aloud a tongue-twister sentence, such as: "Pass the peas, please."
3. Carry out a simple set of instructions, such as: "Take the paper in your hand. Fold it in half. Place it on the chair."
4. Follow simple written instructions, such as: "Clap your hands."
5. Write a sentence on a piece of paper.
6. Copy a design of two intersecting shapes.

Charting My Mother's Decline

We watched my mother struggle to complete the MMSE. But as hard as she tried, my mother couldn't follow the doctor's written or verbal instructions. She couldn't remember a single word the doctor read to her. She couldn't close her eyes as instructed by Dr. Murphy. She just couldn't.

Her embarrassment and frustration were evident as her face turned red, as she laughed and tried to cover up her deficits, and when she furtively looked to us, her eyes pleading for the answers. Her score? Six points ... out of a possible 30. According to Dr. Murphy, my mother was profoundly impaired.

The diagnosis was probable Alzheimer's-type dementia. I say "probable" because Alzheimer's cannot be determined conclusively without an autopsy of the brain (although PET scan technology—positron emission tomography—which measures blood flow and glucose metabolism through the brain, is progressing in this area). Still, a clinical diagnosis—one that includes a complete patient and family history, a physical examination and laboratory tests, psychiatric assessment and neurological testing—can rule out other medical problems, such as drug reactions, stroke, tumors, infections, thyroid problems or nutritional deficiencies that can be treated.

Dr. Murphy talked to us about placement options and treatment protocols. However, I did not hear another thing after he said the word, "Alzheimer's."

I thought I had been prepared for this moment. But even though I knew intellectually that the diagnosis was likely to be Alzheimer's-type dementia, I was overwhelmed by the feelings that flooded my body at that moment. Somehow, I had convinced myself that my mother's condition was caused by a series of strokes, resulting in what is called "infarct dementia." Even that seemed to be a better outcome than a progressively debilitating disease such as Alzheimer's.

As reality began to settle in, an odd mix of grief and relief washed over me. After having lived in limbo for so long, my family now had a common purpose: Marshalling our forces to help

Mom through whatever lay ahead. Getting a diagnosis was the starting point that helped shift our focus.

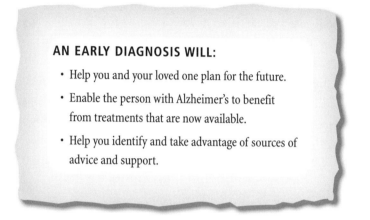

AN EARLY DIAGNOSIS WILL:

- Help you and your loved one plan for the future.
- Enable the person with Alzheimer's to benefit from treatments that are now available.
- Help you identify and take advantage of sources of advice and support.

THE KEYSTONE TO UNDERSTANDING

Getting a diagnosis for your loved one is a crucial stepping stone to finding a path to peace through Alzheimer's. First, it will help you to determine appropriate levels of support and structure for the person with dementia. By learning what behaviors to expect, you can become more flexible when interacting with your loved one.

Second, once you have a name for what is happening, you can begin to adjust your expectations, both of your loved one and of yourself. Adjusting expectations of what your loved one can and cannot do, of what types of activities she can still enjoy, and of what types of assistance she needs, will make it much easier to interact in a positive and supportive way. This was certainly true in my case.

There are many paths to obtaining a diagnosis of dementia, sometimes triggered by an unrelated physical or mental decline or by a previously unheard-of incident of wandering, paranoia, or personal injury. Whatever the nature of your loved one's symptoms, don't delay seeking a diagnosis.

If possible, it is best to consult with a geriatrician—a physician trained specifically in the care of older adults. For ideas on how to locate a geriatrician in your area, see the "Practical Suggestions" at the end of this Chapter.

Obtaining a diagnosis was a turning point for my family. We were finally all on the same page about my mother's future decline. The next step was to look at the legal and financial issues my parents would face as this disease progressed to its inevitable destination.

Suggestions for Expressing and Recording Your Travels:

Receiving a diagnosis of Alzheimer's can trigger a mixture of powerful emotions—positive and negative. What are (or were) some of your fears about this step? Did your fears come true?

_____

_____

_____

_____

_____

Watching my mother struggle through the MMSE was painful. How can you prepare yourself for the medical testing that will be part of your loved one's diagnosis?

_____

_____

_____

_____

_____

"Alzheimer's" is just a word. Whatever illness you are defining, putting a label on it helps to diffuse its power over you and to bring the "word" into focus so that you can deal with the situation more appropriately. How can you redefine "Alzheimer's" so that it supports your personal journey with your loved one?

_____

_____

_____

_____

_____

Practical Suggestions to Help You Pave Your Path:

To locate a doctor who specializes in treating Alzheimer's disease, check with your HMO, primary care physician, friends, and your local Chapter of the Alzheimer's Association or local association for gerontology.

Review your loved one's health insurance policies to determine coverage, requirements for a referral to a geriatrician, availability of specialists in the provider network, co-pays, etc. Contact the insurance carrier with any questions before you visit the doctor.

Prepare for the first visit to the doctor by assembling:
- A medical history;

- The names and dosages of medications (over-the-counter and prescription);
- A copy of your loved one's medical power of attorney;
- A record of symptoms and behaviors; and
- A list of questions to ask the doctor.

FIVE

Complete Legal and Financial Planning

*To have begun is to have done half
the task; dare to be wise.*

HORACE

❀

Family dynamics can be tricky. Each of us occupies a unique place in the pecking order of family life—oldest son, youngest daughter, Daddy's favorite, problem child. Depending on your place in the family, it can be difficult to be heard above the chaos that very often surrounds a devastating diagnosis such as Alzheimer's. But Alzheimer's is an all-consuming disease—for the patient and the family—making it essential that everyone is clear on the goals and challenges of caring for a loved one with dementia. That is why legal and financial planning should begin soon after a diagnosis of Alzheimer's disease is made.

Your loved one may have the capacity to manage his legal and financial affairs right now, but as the disease progresses, that may not continue to be the case. At some point, you or someone else will likely have to act on your loved one's behalf. Advance planning is the key that allows you and your loved one to make decisions together now for whatever may come later.

Early planning can allow your loved one to be involved in the planning process and ensure that his interests and wishes can be respected. It can also ensure that your loved one's money will be wisely managed to help meet the cost of health care, now and in the future.

For my family, completing the necessary legal and financial planning "as soon as possible" meant getting started three years into the journey. It took that amount of time for my father to recognize that he needed to protect my mother in the event that he, nine years her senior, predeceased her. Moving him to this decision, however, wasn't easy.

AN UNEXPECTED LESSON

In 1997, when my mother first started showing signs of memory loss and confusion, I jumped in to convince my family that legal and financial planning was essential. I switched between roles, from daughter to Elder Law attorney, trying to get them to allow me to do for my mother what I had done so often for the clients who had come to my office in search of legal expertise. As I sat in the kitchen, explaining the importance of advance planning, my family stared back at me, skeptical.

I felt as though my expertise as a lawyer was discounted, that they didn't see me as an Elder Law specialist, that they saw me only as the "baby" of the family—the youngest child and little sister who tagged along with nothing to add. My knowledge of legal, financial and community resources was ignored. My voice was quelled.

This was a familiar childhood place for me. I did what I had learned over the years worked best in this type of situation: I remained silent and patiently waited for the right time to try again.

In the meantime, I took action in my office. I tried to make right for my clients what I wasn't allowed to make right at home. I applied what I was learning and feeling as the daughter of an Alzheimer's patient to my Elder Law practice. And that meant bringing a new level of humanity, compassion and patience to my work.

In the past, I had often grown frustrated when clients failed to follow my advice. I had often become impatient when "family dynamics" hampered my ability to advocate for the client. As I waited for my own family's dynamics to play out, however, I began to see how naively I had approached my practice when I would tell family members to *"just work it out."*

When I tried to discuss legal and financial planning for my mother—and hit a brick wall with my family—I came to a startling revelation: The advice I had been doling out to my clients and their families was harder to follow than I had imagined. I realized that my attempt to enforce a time-line to the planning process was disrespectful both to them, and to the process of grieving and acceptance they faced after this diagnosis. As an attorney, I needed to facilitate the planning process—not own it.

To everyone involved, a diagnosis of dementia can feel like walking through quicksand, making slow and steady progress the only pace possible. Among the gifts Alzheimer's offered me was the opportunity to adjust my expectations of my clients and to improve how I conducted my Elder Law practice. I learned the wisdom of the saying, *"it takes as long as it takes"*—assuming, that is, that you don't wait too long to get started!

Connecting early on with an Elder Law attorney will ensure you and your loved one have your legal and financial road map in place for the long journey ahead.

THE WISDOM OF PATIENCE

On the home front, it was only when I stopped pressuring my father that he finally came to me for advice, eventually allowing us to complete the necessary legal and financial planning steps to secure my parents' future. I'm not certain what actually motivated him to seek my counsel, but I am grateful that he did. Perhaps it was my mother's obvious and continual decline. More likely, it was my older sister's influence with him.

She and I had developed a "tag-team" approach to communicating certain issues with our father. Because he seemed more receptive to hearing advice from her, I would suggest an idea to my sister first and she would carry it to Dad. It wasn't the most direct route of communication, but it worked.

Here, too, Alzheimer's opened the door to another gift. Eventually my father softened and allowed me to voice my concerns directly. In the process, I was able to successfully grow up in his eyes. He came to recognize my special expertise as an Elder Law attorney, to hear my concerns and to see the value in letting me help him navigate the legal and financial planning issues facing our family. It felt good to work with him, not as parent and child, but as two adults facing a daunting journey together.

My relationship with my sister also improved along this part of the path as I successfully shed my "little sister" persona. Less than two years separated us in age, yet we were worlds apart in our day-to-day lives and in our thinking about dementia. My sister thought I was "crazy" for viewing and embracing our mother's dementia as a gift. Always the "warrior princess" in our family, her first instinct was to fight this disease with everything she had, physically and emotionally, while I preferred to lie down and let it wash over me.

As we worked together to support our parents, we were able to bridge this gap in our thinking and to rely on our different perspectives to meet the challenges of this journey. Our teamwork approach was one of the new bonds between us, and another gift on my path to peace through Alzheimer's.

LOOK TO THE FUTURE NOW

In many families, it is often an adult child who facilitates the legal and financial planning process and becomes an advocate for the parent in dealing with attorneys and financial planners. Being an "advocate" for your loved one in accomplishing this planning is a very important way to accompany him on his path through Alzheimer's.

Timing is critical in this process. There is no way to back-date time, or to reverse the ravaging effects of a fast-moving dementia if your loved one has lost legal capacity. When this happens, the only available options for financial and personal care planning involve court proceedings known as guardianship and conservatorship. Much of the flexibility available in private legal and financial planning may be lost when a court becomes involved.

As you begin your journey with your loved one, here are some general suggestions to help you address basic legal and financial planning needs. These suggestions are not intended to be legal advice. I encourage you to consult with an Elder Law attorney in your local area regarding the long-term care planning issues faced by you and your loved one.

LEGAL PLANNING

Legal planning for long-term catastrophic illness, such as Alzheimer's, is best done by a specialist known as an "Elder Law" attorney.

Elder Law is a relatively new legal specialty area that has evolved over the last several years and is used to define attorneys who focus on the special needs of older persons and people with long-term illnesses such as Alzheimer's. Their special expertise is aimed at protecting the autonomy, quality of life and financial security of clients as they age or become disabled. This includes preparing for death and disability through "advance directives," estate planning, financial planning to help prepare for the expense of long-term care, including Medicare and Medicaid options and remedying many other issues that may arise during a long-term catastrophic illness.

Planning for the high cost of caring for a loved one with dementia, as well as the emotional and physical demands of caregiving, require the expertise that only a well-trained Elder Law attorney can provide.

Once you decide to engage an Elder Law attorney, he or she must determine the "legal capacity" of the client, particularly if the goal is to prepare and execute advance directives and other documents. This means that the client must have the ability to understand what is going on. Generally speaking, legal capacity may be defined in several different ways depending on the task to be completed. In Colorado, for example, there is a different definition of legal capacity for signing a contract, executing a last will, or making a gift.

It's All About the Right Documents

A large portion of legal planning for the elderly involves the preparation of "advance directives." These are documents that delegate decision-making authority to another person (known as the agent) at a point when the client (known as the principal) is no longer able to make decisions for himself due to mental or physical decline. The beauty of these documents is that they provide a way for your loved one's wishes to be fulfilled even after he can no longer express those wishes himself.

In most cases, the agent is a family member. In cases where there are no family members or there are troublesome family dynamics, the agent can be a third-party professional (also referred to as a "fiduciary").

It is my belief that communication is the foundation upon which effective advance directives rest. That is why I encourage you and your loved one to spend as much time with an attorney as necessary to ensure your understanding of the benefits and limitations of these documents. But remember, time is critical here: Your loved one needs to get together with family members as soon as possible to discuss end-of-life medical decisions and financial decisions to ensure the agent is properly empowered to make the *principal's* decisions when he is unable to do so. If your loved one waits too long to have that discussion, much of the power of the documents to extend his decision-making authority will be lost.

At a minimum, advance directives should include the following three documents:

1. A medical durable power of attorney;
2. A living will; and
3. A general durable power of attorney.

A **medical durable power of attorney** (also referred to as a health care power of attorney) gives the agent the power to make medical decisions on behalf of your loved one, including medical treatments, procedures and services, continued life support, nutrition and hydration, access to medical records, employment of health care personnel, placement, and transportation. In Colorado, a medical durable power of attorney becomes effective when your loved one's treating physician determines that he lacks medical decisional capacity to make these decisions for himself.

A **living will** is a document directing the treating physician how to care for the patient if he is terminally ill and unconscious for a period of time. This document specifies instructions for end of life care. In Colorado, a living will can address the continuation, withholding, or withdrawal of both life sustaining treatments and artificial nutrition and hydration. This information can be included in the medical durable power of attorney, or the living will can be a separate stand-alone document.

A **general durable power of attorney** (also referred to as a power of attorney for property) gives the agent the ability to manage your loved one's financial affairs, including conducting banking transactions, paying bills, filing tax returns, managing business or real property, hiring other professionals, and assisting with financial and legal planning for long-term care. A general durable power of attorney can be effective when it is signed or at some later date when the principal is no longer able to make these decisions for himself.

Advance directives should be tailored to meet the client's needs and wants, and it is recommended that all powers of attorney be "durable." This means that the authority granted to the agent continues beyond the point where the principal is no longer able to direct his own affairs.

Legal planning also includes estate planning, such as drafting wills and trusts to dispose of the client's property at death. Estate planning can be especially important when there is a diagnosis of dementia because there may be special estate planning considerations that go hand-in-hand with the recommended financial planning for long-term care. This inter-relatedness of planning issues is one reason why obtaining legal advice early on, after the diagnosis of dementia, is imperative.

FINANCIAL PLANNING

Alzheimer's is the fourth leading cause of adult death in America today, impacting 4.5 million Americans. The National Institute on Aging (NIA) estimates the overall cost of Alzheimer's at $100 billion a year, with much of that borne by individual families.[7]

While the disease differs from person to person, Alzheimer's is very often a slow-progressing disease with a life expectancy at the time of diagnosis of as many as 10 or even 20 years. Because care in the later stages of this disease can be so expensive, it's essential that you and your loved one begin planning for these financial challenges as soon as a diagnosis is made.

Early planning, which takes into account the preservation

and management of assets, can help ensure your loved one's financial resources are wisely managed so that his or her health-care needs will be properly met, today and in the future. In order to develop such a plan, many families seek the help of professionals who specialize in long-term care issues.

Often this will be a combination of a financial planner, an insurance specialist, and an Elder Law attorney. Together these professionals can help answer the question of how to pay for long-term care without jeopardizing the financial security of the surviving spouse or family members and, where possible, preserve assets for inheritance by future generations. Equally important, having a source for impartial advice about estate planning, trusts and other legal and financial issues may be a source of comfort to the person with Alzheimer's and to the family.

Again, these suggestions are not intended to be legal advice. I strongly recommend that you consult with an Elder Law attorney in your local area regarding the long-term care planning issues faced by you and your loved one.

ORGANIZE YOUR PAPERWORK

Sound financial planning involves a number of steps, beginning with a realistic assessment of your loved one's (and spouse's, if any) financial situation. To determine what funds are currently available and will be in the future, begin collecting and organizing information about your loved one's financial situation. To help you get started, consider the following Financial Planning Checklist:

☐ Bank statements, including checking and savings accounts and investment accounts

- [ ] Brokerage account statements as well as stock, bond and other securities certificates
- [ ] Real estate deeds
- [ ] Insurance policies, including long-term care policies and annuities
- [ ] Disability policies
- [ ] Retirement benefits information (IRA, work-related, private and Social Security)
- [ ] Military benefits information
- [ ] Safe deposit box contents and other valuables
- [ ] Burial plans and plots
- [ ] Automobile titles and values
- [ ] Monthly budget for current care, including the costs for the person with Alzheimer's and the spouse's household budget, if any
- [ ] Copies of existing powers of attorney, last wills, trusts, etc.

With a detailed list of these and other assets, along with supporting documentation, your Elder Law attorney or other long-term care expert can help you and your loved one create a short- and long-term financial plan that takes into account anticipated expenses, spousal support, taxes, asset preservation, and sources of payment for long-term care, such as Medicare, supplemental health insurance, long-term care insurance, Medicaid and other public benefits assistance programs. In particular, it is important to know what long-term care payment options are available so that you can properly plan ahead.

PAYING FOR LONG-TERM CARE

If your loved one is insured, either through an employer or a retirement policy, be sure to read and bring all the policies relating to long-term/progressive illness to your Elder Law attorney. If your loved one is no longer employed and does not have coverage, your Elder Law attorney can help you identify other sources of coverage.

If your loved one is age 65 or older, or is disabled and has paid into the Social Security System through employment deductions for at least 10 years (or 40 quarters), he or she will qualify for **Medicare.** Medicare is a federal health insurance program that is linked to Social Security and Railroad Retirement benefits. Medicare has two parts:

- **Part A** covers inpatient hospital services, limited skilled nursing facility care, home health services, medical supplies and hospice services.

- **Part B** pays 80% of Medicare approved amounts (after the annual deductible is met for outpatient medical services) including doctors and other health care professionals, medically necessary ambulance services, physical, speech and occupational therapy, home health care services (if certified as necessary by a physician), medical supplies and equipment, and outpatient surgery.

What most people do not realize is that Medicare does not typically pay for long-term care in a nursing home. The limited coverage provided by Medicare is for *skilled* nursing services only. It is intended to address acute medical situations which, unlike Alzheimer's, can be cured or improved by short-term daily care or rehabilitation. What the typical patient with dementia requires is "custodial care;" in other words, a place to be kept safe, warm, fed, etc. Unfortunately, this type of *unskilled* care is not covered by Medicare under any circumstances.

If your loved one cannot get insurance and meets certain income and asset thresholds, he or she may be eligible for **Medicaid**. Medicaid is a joint federal-state welfare program that

Long-term care can cost more than $70,000 per year for a private room in a nursing home. Cost varies with the type of coverage purchased and age at time of purchase. Experts recommend that you purchase long-term care insurance in your 40s, when premiums tend to be more affordable. Minimum features to consider include:

- An inflation rider on the daily benefit amount
- Coverage for all levels and locations of care
- Reasonable waiting periods
- Qualification requirements

Be sure to inquire about:

- Pre-existing condition limitations
- Exclusions from coverage
- Waiver of premiums

Finally, it is also important to carefully consider:

- The reputation and financial strength of the issuing insurance company
- Its record of paying benefits
- Its claims processing procedures

pays for medical costs that exceed a person's ability to pay. Its purpose is to provide preventive, therapeutic and remedial health services. Qualifying for Medicaid long term care benefits is a very technical process and eligibility requirements vary from state to state. That is why it is important to seek the advice of a local Elder Law attorney with Medicaid planning experience as soon as possible after a diagnosis of long-term catastrophic illness.

To locate an Elder Law attorney in your area, please see the "Additional Resources" section at the end of this book.

Using **long-term care insurance** to pay for care is another option that many families consider. Keep in mind, long term care insurance is not available once a diagnosis of dementia has been made. However, this should not stop you, as the caregiver, from looking into long term care insurance coverage for yourself.

TIPS FOR CHOOSING AN ELDER LAW ATTORNEY

The legal and financial issues associated with aging and incapacity can be complex and are often interrelated. Choosing an Elder Law attorney who is well versed in these issues will ensure that you and your loved one receive a "holistic" solution to the legal and financial planning issues accompanying a diagnosis of dementia.

The following are some tips that may help you locate the right Elder Law attorney for your needs:

1. **Ask for referrals.** Friends, family physicians and local associations who work with the elderly are all good sources of information about Elder Law attorneys in your area. There are also many referral sources including the National Academy of Elder Law Attorneys, which publishes a nationwide directory of Elder Law attorneys and local associations for other diseases.

The National Academy of Elder Law Attorneys (NAELA) is a non-profit association that assists lawyers, bar organizations and others who work with older clients and their families. NAELA has a free brochure, *Questions and Answers When Looking for an Elder Law Attorney*, which can help you identify the right attorney for your situation. NAELA also has a web site which includes a Member Consumer Registry which can help you locate an Elder Law attorney in your area. See the "Additional Resources" section at the end of this book for more information on how to contact NAELA.

2. **Screen with an initial phone call.** Because of the long-term nature of Alzheimer's, it's important to find an Elder Law attorney with whom you and your loved one are able to communicate, trust and work comfortably over time. Begin your search with an initial phone call. Even if you end up speaking to a secretary, paralegal or office manager during the first call, you can gather important information by asking questions, such as:

- How long has the attorney been in practice?
- What percent of the attorney's practice is devoted to legal issues affecting the elderly?
- What is his or her experience in dealing specifically with Alzheimer's patients?
- What is the cost of an initial consultation?
- Does the attorney make house calls?

- Is the office equipped to handle disabled clients?

- If you decide to make an appointment to learn more, what information should you bring to this meeting?

The answers to these questions will help you begin to evaluate which attorney on your list has the best skills, experience and qualifications to serve you and your loved one's interests.

3. **Meet face-to-face and continue asking questions.** Once you have found an appropriate legal partner, make an appointment for a consultation. Be sure to bring all the information pertinent to your loved one's situation to this meeting. The purpose of this meeting is fact-finding: Your goal is to continue asking questions to make sure you are thoroughly comfortable with your selection. These questions may include:

   - How long it will take to put the proper planning in place?

   - What fees and costs will be involved?

   - What solutions are recommended to address your concerns?

   - If the attorney is part of a group, which one will handle your matter?

   - How will the attorney communicate with you?

4. **Always ask for a written statement of fees and costs.** Attorneys utilize a variety of fee arrangements, including charging by the hour, charging by the document (a "flat fee"), or in some cases, charging a percentage of the value of the case (a "contingent fee"). It is important to understand what types of fees will be charged in your represen-

tation. In addition, many attorneys will charge you for out-of-pocket expenses and some may ask for a retainer.

Whatever the fee plan decided upon with the attorney, however, ask that your arrangement be put in writing. (In Colorado, lawyers are required to provide this.)

5. **Look for an attorney who welcomes the support and involvement of the client's family.** One of the hardest things about practicing Elder Law is determining who the "client" is. Often, consultations with clients are facilitated (and sometimes complicated) by the adult children or other family members whose input is critical to developing a holistic and comprehensive legal and financial plan.

In my practice, I usually take the position that I represent the person with the diagnosis and the spouse, if any. If there is no spouse, then the client may be the adult children or other family members, depending on the legal capacity of the person with dementia.

Armed with a diagnosis and a comprehensive legal and financial plan for my parents, my next step was to build my arsenal of knowledge about Alzheimer's. For me, this meant connecting with my local Chapter of the Alzheimer's Association.

Suggestions for Expressing and Recording Your Travels:

What, if any, barriers are there to your being an advocate for your loved one? Family dynamics? Fear? Lack of commitment? If there are obstacles, what steps can you take to overcome them?

_____

_____

_____

_____

_____

How would you describe the communication patterns in your family? How are these patterns magnified by Alzheimer's?

_____

_____

_____

_____

_____

As a "depression baby" my father had definite ideas about money —ideas that impacted our journey through Alzheimer's. What are the money dynamics of your family? What are *your* money "values"? Do your values conflict or agree with those of your family?

_____

_____

_____

_____

_____

Practical Suggestions to Help You Pave Your Path:

Prepare a monthly budget of expenses to help you weigh your long-term care options. You should be able to "guesstimate" whether your loved one has the resources to stay at home, pay privately for care, or needs public assistance to cover the cost of long-term assisted living or nursing facility care.

Assemble your documents and prepare a list of questions for the attorney before you meet. This will minimize the time and cost and maximize the outcome of your visit.

Contact an insurance broker about long-term care insurance for yourself. To find a broker, check with your existing insurance broker, friends, colleagues, and your local Chapter of the Alzheimer's Association.

SIX

Build a Safety Net

*Though no one can go back and
make a brand new start, anyone can
start from now and make a brand
new ending.*

CARL BARD

❀

For the longest time, my father waged a small battle with my
mother each day. The war zone? My parents' bathroom.

"*Come on, Patty. Stop staring and brush your teeth.*" My father
insisted that my mother was being difficult as she stood frozen in
front of the sink, toothbrush in hand.

I knew better.

My mother wasn't being stubborn or willful. She stared at my
father as if he was speaking a foreign language because, to her, he
was. My mother no longer *knew* what a toothbrush was. Alzheimer's had erased that concept from her brain.

I had seen this kind of behavior many times in my Elder Law
practice: Frustrated family members pleading with a loved one to
remember a word, a face, an activity—something that would give

them hope that Alzheimer's had left something of their loved one's memory intact.

"*Dad it's okay. Give me a second with Mom.*"

I moved closer to my mother, facing the mirror, and handed her the toothbrush. "*Come on Mom, let's brush our teeth.*" Nothing. No response. Then I modeled brushing my own teeth. Without missing a beat, my mother lifted the toothbrush and began to brush her teeth, too. One small victory in the Negri household!

Everything Changes

As Alzheimer's progresses, mental and physical functioning spiral downward. Odd and unexpected behaviors surface, such as wandering or hoarding, or, something my mother did in the beginning, throwing everything in the trash. Elements of personality become exaggerated, such as anger, aggressiveness or possessiveness, creating the potential for increased conflict as family members clash in frustration. Finally, as mental functioning deteriorates, declines in physical skills also can be predicted.

I knew many of these things. As I built my practice, I had worked hard to educate myself about Alzheimer's to better help my clients. But once my mother was diagnosed with this disease, I pro-actively sought out *more* information—this time from the viewpoints of a child and caregiver.

I enrolled in the *"Savvy Caregiver Program"* offered by my local Chapter of the Alzheimer's Association.[8] There, I learned that:

- Dementia is not part of normal aging and may be produced by a number of other diseases or conditions, such as vascular disturbances (i.e., stroke), vitamin and nutritional deficits and alcohol abuse.

- Dementia is a condition of *global* deterioration of memory and cognition, impairing thought and social functioning.

- Dementia may be suspected where there are symptoms, such as serious memory problems, associated with at least one of the following conditions:
  - Difficulty with social functioning,
  - Impairment of abstract thinking, or
  - Disturbances of other thinking processes.

- Typically, dementia is not reversible.

When it comes to caregiving, there is power in sharing. Attending a support group can provide family caregivers with emotional support from other people who are experiencing the same journey. There you can feel safe sharing your feelings in a setting with people who know, firsthand, what you are going through.

The *Savvy Caregiver Program* also taught me what types of mental and physical changes to expect in my mother over time, including:

MEMORY problems, which could include a rapid loss of recent memories combined with a gradual loss of long-term memories. The end result is most memory eventually fades away by the late stage of Alzheimer's. Knowing this helped me to interact more successfully with my mother. It enabled me to accept that many of her social skills had been forgotten, new learning for her was impossible, and her memory was not available to prompt or stimulate action or to orient her to her surroundings. As I grew to understand the limitations imposed on my mother by Alzheimer's, I became more compassionate and patient in helping her to cope with the challenges of daily life.

LANGUAGE problems, which may include difficulty finding words. As the structure of language slowly breaks down, there comes a point where even simple language is lost.

As time went on, my mother's ability to name things completely disappeared. Everything became a "this" or a "that," making communication increasingly problematic, especially when it came to determining her needs. Eventually, she lost all of her words. It finally occurred to me to rely not on language but on childlike intuition to "read" her behaviors, to anticipate her needs, and to find the missing words for her. Tapping into my inner child's wisdom was one of the ways I reconnected with myself along this journey.

For example, I knew that my mother often used the opposite word for what she really meant. If she said the water was too cold when I washed her hair, I knew she meant it was too hot. I also knew that correcting her misspoken words could become confrontational, and so I avoided doing this with her as much as possible. Pausing before reacting helped me to get in touch with my inner wisdom and refocus my attention on my mother's needs, not her limitations.

REASONING problems, which result from a breakdown in the connection between thoughts, objects, events and actions. As Alzheimer's progresses, the behavior of the demented individual becomes more random, impulsive and self-centered, and no amount of reasoning will adjust the behavior. As a result, you may find that your loved one increasingly makes poor choices, particularly with regard to safety issues.

Safety is an area where it is particularly important to become pro-active in assuming responsibility, regardless of your loved one's objections. In my practice, for example, I see many families struggle with the issue of how to tell the Alzheimer's patient that he or she should no longer drive.

HOW DO YOU STOP YOUR LOVED ONE FROM DRIVING?

This is a difficult issue for many families. The Alzheimer's Association recommends that you:

- Encourage the person to voluntarily stop driving;
- Ask your loved one's physician for support;
- Make the car less accessible (take away the keys, disable the car, park it elsewhere);
- Request the department of motor vehicles to have the license revoked; or
- Have a driving assessment completed by the department of motor vehicles, AAA, or your local rehabilitation hospital.

Be reassuring but firm — avoid long explanations and focus on other activities that your loved one can still enjoy.

BEHAVIORAL problems, including paranoia and suspicion, which result as your loved one loses the ability to interpret and understand the actions of others. In this impaired state, your loved one may become easily overwhelmed and take refuge in blame.

For example, many Alzheimer's patients accuse their loved ones of abuse, abandonment, theft and trickery. This can be devastating for concerned family members and caregivers who, taking the accusations personally, feel they have no choice but to withdraw as a caregiver or, alternatively, to take over the person's life completely with a court action, such as a guardianship or conservatorship. (These are court proceedings that appoint someone to make medical or financial decisions for another, and are often more restrictive alternatives than powers of attorney.)

As my mother's Alzheimer's progressed, she grew increasingly wary of any private conversation that went on around her. For example, if she "caught" me talking with my father, she immediately grew agitated, demanding to know what we were discussing. Eventually, she wouldn't let him out of her sight.

PROBLEM SOLVING becomes a challenge for the Alzheimer's patient, who progressively loses the familiar concepts of time, space and relationship. The person can become entrenched in concrete thinking, making abstract thought impossible. You may find that your loved one loses attention easily and becomes more and more disorganized—one reason why ongoing structure and support are crucial to a person with Alzheimer's daily life. Confusion and agitation are common mental states.

With my mother, I found by making slight adjustments in my own behavior, such as slowing down my movements and speech, maintaining eye contact or touch with her at all times when we were in a public place, and by using humor, I was able to hold her attention longer and lower her anxiety levels considerably.

For example, my mother had several foot problems. As Alzheimer's progressed, she also lost her ability to tie shoe laces. So, upon the recommendation of her doctor, my sister and I tried to assist her with finding new slip-on shoes. I took her to three different stores. She was obstinate in not wanting to remove her threadbare tennis shoes. I would ask her to raise her foot so I could take off her shoe, and she would refuse. No amount of reasoning that the corn on her foot and the resulting pain and limited mobility could be alleviated by new shoes, would convince her to give up control of her feet or to part with her tattered shoes.

As I sat on the floor of the third store, surrounded by several mismatched shoes, I alternated between cajoling her, pleading with her and scolding her, all to no avail. In the end, she just walked away from me and said, *"Let's go home now."* So home we went. But I knew we would try again the next Tuesday and this time hopefully I could persuade her to lift her feet.

PHYSICAL FUNCTIONING also is impacted by the various stages of dementia. Gait and balance deteriorate over time, and falls become a worrisome risk. Incontinence of bowel and bladder are commonplace. The ability to initiate behaviors may be impaired, making constant reminders and structured support necessary just to accomplish basic tasks of daily living.

One particular area of physical functioning which becomes troublesome for many Alzheimer's patients and their caregivers is personal hygiene. Often, it is one of the first things the demented mind leaves behind. Likewise, coordinated wardrobe ensembles may be discarded along the journey, in favor of mismatched pieces and multiple layers inappropriate to the season. Underwear may go missing in the daily uniform of the demented. The same clothes can be worn daily for weeks at a time, even substituting for pajamas. Struggling with bathing can seem like an impossible task, particularly with a modest person, like my mother. When bathing becomes a contentious issue, many families opt for out-of-home placement.

The theories behind why a demented person loses all sense of personal cleanliness and order are many, and may include depression, changed perception of water temperatures, fear of

The *Savvy Caregiver Program* teaches participants to consider how the following three components affect the person's ability to perform any given task:

- The size and complexity of the task to be performed — e.g., how many steps are involved?
- The structure of the task — how is the task set up for the person with dementia?
- The level of support — how can the caregiver instruct, guide, encourage, and keep the person with dementia on track?

water, loss of privacy and loss of independence with assisted bathing. Or it may be as simple as losing an understanding of what bathing is, the many steps involved and why it is important to bathe regularly.

LETTING GO OF THE "SHOULDS"

The knowledge I gained from the Alzheimer's Association helped me to become a more competent companion and caregiver as I journeyed with my mother on this path. Equally important, this knowledge helped me to neutralize my own negative reactions to the changes brought on by my mother's disease, helping me to become more comfortable "expecting the unexpected" from her.

With this understanding, I was able to let go of my notion of "how things should be" and, instead, learned to focus on living in the present moment with "how things really were." This shift in thinking helped me to cope with, and ultimately negate, many unproductive emotions that swirled inside me, including my overwhelming feelings of anger, anxiety and guilt. Expecting the unexpected also helped me to stop blaming myself when something I did seemed to trigger a negative reaction in my mother. This powerful tool was an important stepping stone on my path to peace—one that I might not have found without the help of outside support from organizations like the Alzheimer's Association.

Getting in touch with the Alzheimer's Association and other local support organizations that provide services to Alzheimer's patients and caregivers is fundamental to helping you cope with the stresses involved with this devastating disease. These organizations provide ongoing education and support groups to assist you, most of which are free of charge. The classes they offer and the groups they sponsor can help you understand and prepare for the emotional changes and logistical challenges that often accompany this disease. See the list of National Resources for Caregivers on page 158.

THINK AHEAD, JUST IN CASE

Even families that intend to keep their loved one at home should become familiar with the various support groups and resources available in their community. Advance preparation will allow you to take advantage of these resources in the event of an emergency and help you to plan ahead for some much-needed break from caregiving. The Alzheimer's Association can provide a list of resources in your town or surrounding area, including the names of respite providers, adult day care facilities, assisted living homes and nursing homes.

The power of these resources to help cannot be overstated. Learning as much as possible about Alzheimer's can help you adjust your expectations so that they are in line with where your loved one actually is in terms of functionality. This, in turn, can help you more successfully interact in your time together.

For me, education also provided an unexpected benefit: It helped me to transform how I related to myself. Learning as much as I could about dementia was the foundation of how I navigated this new and unfamiliar territory with my mother. The next step was to turn my focus inside and to ask myself the question, *"How do I prepare myself for this journey?"*

Suggestions for Expressing and Recording Your Travels:

Expectations can create our reality if we let them. What are some of your unrealistic expectations of your loved one with dementia? Of yourself as you accompany your loved one on this journey? What can you do to bring your expectations into line with where your loved one actually is?

_____

_____

_____

_____

_____

Can you look back at some instances with your loved one when you became impatient, angry, or frustrated, and see how you owned these emotions? If the situation were to happen again, how might you react differently?

_____

_____

_____

_____

_____

How can learning more about dementia help you to avoid these negative behaviors in the future? What do you need to learn about and how will you go about finding this knowledge?

_____

_____

_____

_____

_____

Practical Suggestions to Help You Pave Your Path:

Make a list of your personal support system, including your friends, clergy, colleagues, family, neighbors, case manager, local Alzheimer's Association, etc. Have this list handy for emergencies.

Review the list of mental and physical changes that are part of the various stages of Alzheimer's at page 11, and begin to catalog your loved one's current status with each item. Track changes as the disease progresses. This will help you to adjust your expectations of your loved one's abilities over time.

Identify and contact your local Chapter of the Alzheimer's Association. Sign up to receive their monthly newsletter and class listing. Learn what support services are available to you. Attend a "Getting Started" program.

SEVEN

How Do I Prepare Myself for this Journey?

My fellow Americans, I have recently been told that I am one of the millions of Americans who will be afflicted with Alzheimer's disease. Upon learning this news, Nancy and I had to decide whether as private citizens we would keep this a private matter or whether we would make this news known in a public way... So now, we feel it is important to share it with you. In opening our hearts, we hope this might promote greater awareness of this condition. Perhaps it will encourage a clearer understanding of the individual and families who are affected by it...

RONALD REAGAN
Former President
Letter to America, November 5, 1994

❀

After my mother was diagnosed with Alzheimer's and the reality began to set in, I started to tell my friends and colleagues what was happening. As you might expect, nearly every one expressed sympathy. They offered friendship, concern, condolences—the very same gestures of friendship I would have offered had our roles been reversed.

So why did their generous offers of comfort make me feel so uneasy?

In the great *"Is the glass half empty or half full?"* debate, my friends and I were on opposite sides. They saw my mother's disease as a terrible tragedy. I saw it as an opportunity for learning and personal growth. Is it any wonder that, when I told my friends I viewed my mother's dementia as one of the greatest gifts she had given me, they looked at me with a mixture of shock and disbelief?

"A gift? Kathleen, you've got to be kidding. Your Mom is going to lose her memory. Before long, she won't even remember who you are."

As if I wasn't already painfully aware of my mother's prognosis! The prospect of losing my mother was heartbreaking to me. But that wasn't the point. I would not have wished Alzheimer's on anyone, let alone my mother. But once she was diagnosed with this dreadful disease, I became doggedly determined to make the best of the situation, to mine the opportunities for personal growth and forgiveness Alzheimer's might provide to me.

Here's how I came to see it: Alzheimer's is a family disease. Of course, dementia alters only the landscape of the patient's brain. But the truth is, dementia also profoundly alters the lives of those who love and care for the Alzheimer's patient.

I could choose to let Alzheimer's drain me of vitality and rob me of my peace of mind. Or, I could choose a different path— one where I used my mother's disease as a catalyst to bring us closer and to heal the childhood wounds that had previously kept me from loving my mother more fully. Instinctively and without hesitation, I chose to make Alzheimer's a path to peace—instead of letting myself become another victim in Alzheimer's minefield of loss.

That is how I came to embrace my journey through Alzheimer's and the myriad hidden and unexpected gifts in my mother's disease—starting with the opportunity to recast the relationships I traditionally had with my mother, my family and, ultimately, with myself and my world.

I was determined to see my mother's illness from a new perspective. I wanted to find a way to take control of the experience for myself, and this meant just one thing to me—*thinking* differently about dementia.

I Could Change Only Myself

Through trial and error, I quickly figured out that I could not change the diagnosis or what this disease process would likely do to my mother. I could not alleviate her anger or fear as she dealt with her fate. I could not change my father's reluctance to make what I felt were the appropriate choices regarding her medical care. I could not convince my siblings to trust that my expertise on aging issues would show them the "right way" to proceed. I finally recognized that I could not control anything or anyone except myself to make this a rewarding and constructive process for me.

Realizing this, I came back to myself, where I had the opportunity to become empowered; to fashion my own reality about dementia. And, it was here, by focusing my attention on myself and my thoughts, and by giving myself permission to feel everything—all my healthy and unhealthy emotions—I grew better equipped to accompany my mother on her journey through Alzheimer's. It was here I found a path of love and connection.

All of this started when I asked myself this question: *"How do I prepare myself for this journey?"* This question—both simple and complex—became the second stepping stone on my path to peace through Alzheimer's. As I looked inward for an answer, my life opened up with possibility.

I have long been a student of the philosophy which says, *"thinking makes it so."* My companion and facilitator in these studies has been Rosa Mazone, a well-known speaker, consultant and educator on the issues of self-discovery and empowerment. I have learned that what I think—my beliefs both conscious and unconscious, my attitudes, point of view, state of mind, and ideas—create how I feel. And how I feel creates my reality—the behaviors and circumstances that surround me are the direct result of my feelings. I am responsible for the outcomes of my life; it is not what happens, but my interpretation of what happens, that either delights or upsets me.

Thinking back to when I first told my friends about my mother's diagnosis, there were many words I could have used to explain what was happening to my mother. I chose the word, *"journey."* Sure, that is not the typical word used to describe this disease. But characterizing her decline into dementia as a "journey" was a way for me to positively give voice to what was happening—one that also allowed me to become an active participant with her.

My thinking was this: If my mother was on a journey, I could accompany her. If she was in the process of dying, however, I could not go with her. I wanted to be her *companion* through her disease and so I came to view Alzheimer's as a journey instead of a destination.

Making this choice to think positively about what was clearly a devastating set of circumstances did not change the outcome. However, it did change how I felt and acted in relation to the possibilities. It was in that choice that I took control of this experience for myself. It was also how, by truly understanding that I alone was responsible for my thoughts, feelings and outcomes, I learned to take blame out of the equation of my adult life.

Updating My "Dictionary of Life"

This is not to say that I changed my thinking overnight. I didn't. Like everyone else, I had been soaking up the beliefs and attitudes of those around me, starting from childhood on. Many of those thought patterns—about my mother, disease, commitment, obligation and self worth—initially got in the way of my finding a path to peace through Alzheimer's. I had my very own "dictionary of life" which I needed to rewrite in order to uncover the ways in which my assumptions about my mother and my place in our family served or defeated my strong desire to change.

Facing down the long and frightening path of dementia with my mother, I saw many ways in which my dictionary needed editing. Walking down this path with her, feeling bad much of the time, I experienced first hand the results of my "stinking thinking." The words and definitions I had for living needed to be updated to support me along this journey. Only I could give this gift to myself.

Alzheimer's is a life-changing disease—for the patient and for the family. What can you do to prepare yourself for the journey ahead? Rosa Mazone taught me a simple, yet powerful, five-step process that helped me to revise my dictionary of life. Perhaps these steps will help you also find your power on this path.

HOW CAN YOU PREPARE YOURSELF FOR THIS JOURNEY?

1. Make an inventory of your thoughts.

2. Identify the sources of your thoughts.

3. Change your negative interpretations.

4. Practice. Practice. Practice.

5. Support your new thoughts with knowledge.

STEP 1: Make an Inventory of Your Thoughts

First, I tuned into my own self-talk, the never-ending voice inside my head that guided my every move, and learned to listen without judgment. As I wrote down my thoughts, I asked myself: How do I feel about my mother?

- My mother was always distant.
- I can't remember being hugged.
- She rarely said, "*I love you.*"
- Mom was always busy cleaning house.

Next, I asked myself: How do I feel about losing my mother?

- Will I miss her?
- Will I ever stop feeling angry?
- Was it too late to mend fences?

Then, I thought about aging.

- Drooling.

- Walkers.

- Depends.

- I wondered: Could I watch my "Audrey Hepburn mother" grow old before her time?

The process of writing the answers to these kinds of questions helped me to identify whether my thoughts were positive or negative, supportive or critical. Recording these thoughts helped me to see more clearly and to test my expectations versus the reality of my situation.

With my list in hand, I tested each thought to be sure it was my truth and not someone else's. For each thought I asked myself:

- How does this thought serve me?

- If I acted on this thought, what would be the result for me?

- Does this thought support my goals for my mother and me?

Making an inventory of my thoughts about my role on this journey, I was able to identify several deeply-held beliefs from my childhood that were at the root of my discomfort with my mother. Once I did this, it became much easier to change my attitudes and my behavior—and to forge a new, healthier bond with her.

STEP 2: Identify the Sources of Your Thoughts

Identifying the sources of your thoughts is a critical step to understanding why you may become so entrenched in negative thinking about this journey with your loved one. As I reflected on some of my negative views about disease and aging, I saw that some originated in my early childhood. These were the deepest and most challenging to rework. Other thoughts were relatively new, coming from my professional career.

During my practice as an Elder Law attorney, I heard every horrible story there was to tell about dementia and its impact on families, stories of dysfunctional dynamics that literally destroyed families. I found many of these stories making their way into my thinking about my mother. They caused me to feel overwhelmed with negative and fearful thoughts about this journey with her. Other powerful sources of my thoughts included what I heard from my family, teachers, friends, colleagues, and from religious and cultural influences.

In the confusion of these many voices, I had to sort through which of these beliefs and ideas was really true about my situation with my mother and my family. It was imperative to find and

It might be said that there is only one all-encompassing need— for love. This view has been eloquently expressed by Frena Gray-Davidson on the basis of her experience as a carer. She asserts that people with dementia often show an undisguised and almost childlike yearning for love. By this she means a generous, forgiving and unconditional acceptance, a wholehearted emotional giving, without any expectation of direct reward. The presence of dementia, she suggests, may provoke a psychospiritual crisis in family members: 'If we do not deal with our own issues of love, and grief around the failures of love, we cannot live with Alzheimer's disease.'

TOM KITWOOD

follow my inner truth, as this was what I would rely on in the difficult times that lay ahead with my mother. I firmly believed the meaning I gave to each situation on this journey was crucial and of my choosing.

STEP 3: Change Your Negative Interpretations

When I learned to listen to my own inner voice, I finally gave myself permission to feel *all* of my feelings along this journey. Listening allowed me to fully embrace both my healthy and unhealthy feelings, knowing that each one had some truth to tell me about my thinking. I often asked myself: What was I feeling as I traveled this path with my mother?

It's true, my mother had been a distant and reserved parent. She hadn't spent a lot of time nurturing me, physically or emotionally. She had been more interested in keeping our house clean than spending time relating to me. How could I open my heart to her when hers had seemed closed to me for so many years?

Along this journey, I felt guilty, helpless, angry. But mostly, I felt sad. There were moments when my negative feelings overwhelmed me, when I found myself reliving the pain and loneliness of my childhood. I felt justified in my resentment—until one day I looked at the evidence before me. Alzheimer's had unlocked my mother's personality. No longer distant and reserved, she became warm and loving. She had changed. And now, it was my turn to change.

Pulling together these three pieces of information—my thoughts, the sources of my thoughts and my interpretations— showed me just how tightly the very fabric of my mother-daughter relationship was wound around my childhood wounds. I realized that working to heal and release these wounds would be a major goal of my companion journey.

When I made a commitment to accompany my mother on this journey, I accepted this challenge. Furthermore, sorting through my catalog of thoughts and feelings highlighted the connections between them and the underlying patterns of my *entire* life, not just in this new place of having a mother with dementia. In what other places and with what other people did I apply the same patterns of unhealthy thinking? I realized that it was time to work on changing the basics of how I saw myself and the world around me.

Recognizing and embracing your emotional responses to various situations and connecting these feelings to your thoughts are vital to taking control of your experience, too. You have the power to change your perception by altering your thinking. Feeling bad is simply the signal that you are interpreting the situation negatively. *Welcome feeling bad.* Let that feeling remind you that you have control of the experience and the power to adjust your thinking.

Step 4: Practice. Practice. Practice.

Like any new skill, it takes practice to replace negative thoughts with positive ones before they are fully integrated into your daily routine. This takes time and patience, repetition and reprogramming. Think about how many years it took for you to create your dictionary of "stinking thinking" and be gentle and supportive in your new role as editor.

I used many methods to actively integrate my new thinking in my daily life. I developed the habit of monitoring my self-talk, rooting out the negative thoughts, and replacing them with positive thoughts. There were many ways of doing this. For example,

- I posted affirmation cards in my house and my car to remind me:

- Be patient. Mom doesn't remember how to brush her teeth.

- Be forgiving. Dad is lost too.

- Be gentle with myself. Alzheimer's takes a toll on all of us.

- I bought a journal—and I wrote in it every day, using Rosa Mazone's format to reprogram my dictionary of life, with the mantra: "I used to think _____, and now I realize that _____."

- I took my new dictionary around with me as I interacted with others. I focused on talking positively about my mother and her disease, sharing with friends and colleagues what I wished for myself and for my mother. I incorporated the words "journey" and "gift" into my conversations, as I learned to talk freely and with love about my mother's illness to others:

  - *"I had a great walk with Mom this morning."*

  - *"We spent nearly an hour laughing over old photos and love letters."*

  - *"We had fun today."*

- I translated my new dictionary into new behavior. I learned from my past "mistakes," those instances when I "felt bad" as I interacted with my mother, and practiced adjusting my thinking and my behavior. I saw more clearly the many ways my behavior towards my mother was a mirror of how she had mothered me. I practiced putting my own personality aside and just being with my mother in the moment.

This wasn't easy at first. I carried almost 40 years of history and pain with me. It was so tempting and so easy to become bogged down with the past, to ignore that our relationship had really changed. Each day I worked on changing my thoughts bit by bit.

The more I did these things, the more I started to live the positive feelings I had been trying to create. Over time, I changed my negative thinking about the hopelessness of dementia. I realized I could contribute positively to my mother's life. I also realized I had much good to learn from this experience and from her. There were hidden gifts and opportunities for transformation on this journey. I would find them if I paid attention and stayed in the present moment with my mother.

As I shifted my thinking to this positive perspective, it naturally became easier to spend time with my mother and to continue the process of healing the childhood wounds I ascribed to her. This was the exact place I needed to be!

Step 5: Support Your New Thoughts with Knowledge

Finally, I learned all I could about my mother's disease.

- I read the latest articles.
- I attended classes at my local Chapter of the Alzheimer's Association.
- I talked with her doctor about new drugs.
- I networked with others coping with Alzheimer's.

The more I learned, the better I could match my steps to my mother's needs. This made it easier for me to spend time with her—to minimize her agitation and to find joy in our moments together.

Knowledge is the sturdiest foundation you will find for supporting your new thinking strategies. Sometimes, a lack of knowledge on a particular subject, or believing in a myth about dementia, can be the source of your negative thinking. For example, knowledge helped me come to a place of understanding where I could more clearly see that I could not change the situation for my mother or her ability to fully comprehend what was happening to her.

Knowledge of the stages of dementia helped guide me in determining appropriate levels of support and structure for my mother so our time together minimized her agitation and maximized her enjoyment. Familiarizing myself with the behaviors of the various stages of dementia helped me to adopt the habit of expecting the unexpected from my mother and to become a more competent caregiver for her on this path.

Knowledge also taught me I was the one who needed to adjust my thinking, my behavior, and my expectations of both of us. I was the only one who could change in our relationship. In the end, knowledge helped me to drop my concept of perfectionism and to find ways to bring compassion to this journey with my mother. This was a journey of tough choices—but I always came back to the truth that I was the only person in this relationship who could change, and therefore, I owned the outcome.

This five-step process for taking control of my experience with Alzheimer's fortified me to think more positively about my mother's dementia and to see what was happening to her as a journey of new discoveries. I defined each loss of her as a potential gift for me. I discovered endless opportunities for transforming my relationships. This positive mind-set became my faith as I traveled this journey with her. Keeping this faith helped me to be in a place of peace and alignment, allowing me to remain capable of hope and love every day as I accompanied her on this final journey.

By taking control of the experience for myself, I was emotionally prepared to move on to the next stage of my personal journey with the assurance it would be positive for me. I was ready to ask the final question on my path to peace, *"How can I stay open to the gifts this experience has to offer?"* It was time to put my knowledge from the experts together with my knowledge of myself and to begin uncovering the hidden gifts and opportunities for transformation on this journey with my mother.

Suggestions for Expressing and Recording Your Travels:

What traditional roles did you play in your family? How are these roles playing out now as you accompany your loved one on this journey? What steps can you take to change any negative patterns that play out in your family today?

_____

_____

_____

_____

_____

Do you have any "stinking thinking?" What are some of the negative thoughts that you hold onto about yourself? Your loved one? Alzheimer's? Aging? How do these thoughts serve you? What would happen if you just started letting them go?

_____

_____

_____

_____

Choose one of your negative thoughts and practice changing your interpretation of the situation. Write an affirmation card with your new positive thought and review it several times each day. How does it feel to change your thoughts?

_____

_____

_____

_____

_____

Practical Suggestions to Help You Pave Your Path:

Buy a journal and make it your special place to record your thoughts. You may want to include favorite pictures or quotes as inspiration for your writings.

Schedule regular times to be with yourself on this journey. Mark times out on your work or personal calendar. Keep these dates to process your experience.

Talk with your siblings and other relatives to see what their thoughts are about this process. Compare their thoughts to your own. This may help you to identify family patterns and also fortify your positive thinking.

EIGHT

How Can I Stay Open to the Gifts this Experience has to Offer?

When I let go of what I am, I become what I might be. When I let go of what I have, I receive what I need.

LAO-TZU

"Today, 70 percent of the 4.5 million Americans with Alzheimer's disease live at home where family and friends provide most of their care... The more families are involved in caring for people with dementia in residential care settings the greater the likelihood of improved individual care and resident well being."[9]

It is my belief that to have a successful journey with your loved one—to experience the numerous hidden gifts and transformations along the way—you must make a commitment to spend regular time together. It was along this part of the path that I discovered a new definition for my self worth and reinvented my role on this journey—and where I transformed from the invisible child into the very visible advocate!

The greater the amount of face time you have with your loved one, the more opportunities there will be for you to experience your own personal growth on this journey. That's because it is typically in the quiet time of ongoing contact that pathways of communication are (re)discovered, prophesies are revealed, and new connections are made. Also, there will inevitably come a time when your loved one will no longer recognize you. Thus, making a commitment to spend regular time early on will be precious for both of you.

To fully experience and appreciate the changes dementia made to my mother's hard-wiring and what this meant to our relationship and to receive the many gifts she had to offer, I had to be present and interact with her on a regular basis. Otherwise, I would have missed much of what she had to share with me on this final journey. Luckily, my mother lived close to me so I could see her regularly. If your loved one lives far away, it may be more of a challenge for you to establish regular communication. Check with your local Chapter of the Alzheimer's Association for information on how to maintain a long-distance connection with your loved one.

Above all else, the reconsideration of dementia invites us to a fresh understanding of what it is to be a person.

TOM KITWOOD

I believe that any amount of regular time with your loved one is the key, with quality more important than quantity. It did not take a commitment of hours and hours to connect with my mother, nor in my case, did it require a complete reorganization of my life. I decided to visit my mother each Tuesday morning for two to three hours starting in June 2001 up until her death in July 2004. Whatever schedule you set up, find what works for you and your loved one.

Tuesdays with Mom

When I first started going to see my mother, I found I was often distracted, my attention divided between my life and hers; in particular, the demands of my work would intrude on our time together. I'd leave her feeling disengaged and drained—the opposite of my goal of accompanying her on this journey.

But here's what I learned as the weeks continued: It takes practice to stay in the moment when your loved one has Alzheimer's—to put their needs ahead of yours. By setting and keeping to a schedule of weekly visits, I had the framework I needed to shift my focus away from my life and into hers for those few hours every week. I also made another powerful choice in my life: To shed the stresses of my own life so that I could remain open to my mother in our time together.

Clearing your mind and remaining focused isn't always easy, especially with the demands most of us face at work and at home. Some people find it helps to say an affirmation before visiting their loved one; others remain mindful through practice and patience. However you manage to retrain your thoughts, it is well worth the effort to keep yourself totally present whenever you're with your loved one (more about this in Chapter 10).

Being consistent with the timing of my visits also benefited my parents. They knew they could expect me to arrive every Tuesday morning around 9:00 and stay until around 11:30. By keeping to a regular schedule, my father was able to plan some much-needed time away from home and his duties as caregiver, and in the summer months he was able to pursue his favorite leisure activity, fishing. Keeping a regular schedule also provided the necessary structure to plan outings for my mother, like lunch dates with friends or trips to favorite shopping spots. Finally, regularity also helped my mother to focus on Tuesday mornings as a special time just for her, and she came to anticipate my visits, which made me feel good!

How did I make the shift in thinking necessary to give my mother the focus she deserved? I developed a weekly exercise, an active "meditation" that helped me to retrain my thoughts when I was with her and prepared me to be with her fully and completely. My meditation, grounded in the thinking strategies of Chapter 7 included four steps:

1. Leave my own agenda at home;

2. Let go of the past with my mother;

3. Reveal my true self to her; and

4. Pay attention to my mother as if she was a prophet.

Constantly working through these four steps was an important catalyst for my personal growth on this journey with my mother. I no longer allowed my thoughts to wander away from my mother during our visits. I remained totally focused on my mother and our time together. For the first time in my life, I began to see her clearly as an *individual* and not just a mother. Interestingly, after a few months of this practice, I found this meditation was energizing for me in all the relationships of my life—another one of the hidden gifts I found as I traveled the path with my mother through Alzheimer's.

Some of my friends wondered, *"How can you afford to take time away from your busy practice?"* The irony was my income and work opportunities weren't diminished by this "away time." What actually happened was that my work flow changed to accommodate this commitment. The fewer hours I devoted to work each week became more productive and enriching for me. Additionally, the compassion and insight I developed as a result of this away time also benefited my Elder Law practice—I learned to adjust my expectations of my clients and I brought a new sense of compassion, patience, and understanding to my work.

Thus, making a commitment to spend regular time with my mother benefited me in ways that I had not imagined or considered. Now, the question became: Could I get out of my own way and make this a peaceful journey for both of us?

Suggestions for Expressing and Recording Your Travels:

When you think about making a commitment to spend regular time with your loved one, what obstacles or emotions arise? Do you become nervous? Resentful? Fearful? What thoughts are motivating you to feel this way?

_____

_____

_____

_____

_____

What impact does time play in your decision? Finding time in your schedule to be with your loved one may not be as difficult as you believe—especially when you recognize that it is quality, not quantity that counts.

_____

_____

_____

_____

_____

What would be the benefits of spending regular time with your loved one? As you think about how you would spend this time, consider making fun a part of your visit with your loved one.

_____

_____

_____

_____

_____

Practical Suggestions to Help You Pave Your Path:

Discuss with your own family and your employer your desire to make a regular time commitment to your loved one. Look for ways to combine efforts so that you can find extra time for this commitment.

Consider how you can involve the other members of your family in the care and companionship of your loved one. Ask for the help you need and want.

What were the strengths of your relationship with your loved one before Alzheimer's moved in. Look for ways that you can build on those strengths in the challenging days ahead.

NINE

Leave Your Own Agenda
at Home

*There will come a time when you
believe everything is finished. That
will be the beginning.*

LOUIS L'AMOUR

❁

When I first started visiting my mother on Tuesday mornings, I
thought I had to structure my time, to make it *useful* and to help
my father around the house. Thus, I arrived with my own agenda
for the visit—a list of chores I decided was important. I
approached my time with my mother as a set of tasks to be completed around the house, like the fact that my parents' once
immaculate house was now in total disarray—and it was *my* job
to clean it.

Each Tuesday, after I had left the house, my mother would yell
at my father, accusing me of taking over her house. This greatly
upset my father, although he never mentioned this to me. Instead,
he told my sister about our mother's tirades. When I learned what

was happening from my sister, I felt angry and ashamed, misunderstood and self righteous, and unappreciated.

In the end, this "wake-up call" was good. Feeling bad triggered the alarm clock in my head—the one that told me something in my thinking was awry. I knew then that I needed to look carefully at my choices and reconsider the definitions I had of self worth, love and acceptance, and to rethink my role in this journey. And so I undertook the slow, painstaking process of adjusting my thinking, editing my "dictionary of life," to put myself on a healthier path—one where I would eventually grow to become wiser and stronger emotionally.

Having the ability to 'be present' is a gift to other people, and it is a kind of liberation for oneself. It means being less troubled about the past, less fearful about the future, and thus more centered on what is immediately at hand. 'Being present' entails letting go of that obsession with doing which often damages care work, and having a greater capacity simply for being.

TOM KITWOOD

BACK TO THE DRAWING BOARD

I began to inventory my thoughts about my various roles in this dementia process, including my roles as daughter, sister, lawyer, caregiver and advocate. As a result of this analysis, I saw how confused I was in assessing my place in my mother's journey.

Each role was defined by my "doing;" by the ways in which I felt I could be helpful, lighten the load on my father, cover up the loss of my mother around the house, and complete the necessary legal and financial planning for my parents. What I realized is that I equated "doing" with love. After all, this was how I had been raised.

For example, I believed if the house was spotless my mother was not lost; that somehow I could put her back together again if I could keep her house clean. I wanted to fix all of this for her. I was wrong.

Looking back, it was easy to see why I was so completely entrenched in my thinking. I had learned as a child to define my worth by output, my love by the things I did for others. Instead of using words and touch, my parents and their parents did things for me. This was how they expressed their love. Was it any wonder that I felt as though I could never do enough for my family to win their love in return?

As I worked through this inventory of my thoughts—the sources of my behavior—I realized I had become entangled in yet another one of the many role reversals my mother and I eventually shared on this journey: That of becoming a protective parent to my parent. By imposing my agenda upon my mother, however well intentioned, I was mirroring her parenting role with me as a child. I was turning our relationship into a series of tasks to be completed, this time according to my schedule, not hers.

Doing vs. Being

The problem was, when I was "doing," instead of feeling, I was also ignoring what was really going on for my mother. Knowing my mother's absolute dedication to her house, it occurred to me that despite her disease, she still needed to believe she was in control of her world, that she captained her household just as before. As I scrubbed, polished and dusted her home, was I inadvertently erasing this important part of my mother's identity?

With this realization, it became easier for me to see why my mother was threatened by my actions: She saw my help with household chores as a denial of her very existence. It was no longer possible for me to justify my actions. It was time to change my interpretation of my role in this process.

Changing my definition of my role from *doing* to *being* wasn't easy for me to accomplish. However, my mother unexpectedly became a role model for me to make this change.

As I looked carefully at the changes in my mother, I witnessed how dementia had set her free of her definition of self worth. Alzheimer's had erased her ability to do, leaving her to thrive in this new place of being. I realized that my mother's dementia presented me with the opportunity to set myself free of this definition, too.

I began my transformation by reminding myself of why I was spending time with my mother in the first place. I wanted to accompany her, to be a companion for her. Imposing my agenda on her was not part of this original plan—it had crept in because of my own personality, my own hard-wiring, much of which had been programmed by my mother in the first place. Furthermore, if I was truly committed to spending time *with* my mother, then I needed to free myself of the memories and emotions blocking my ability to connect anew. Taking this step provided me with yet another pathway for my transformation.

And so, I put away the broom. I walked past the piles of clothes. I resisted the temptation to dust surfaces or to sort through and discard piles of newspapers, magazines and mail. I stopped looking under beds and into toilet bowls for evidence of neglect. Instead, I just sat down, face to face, to be with my mother. I stopped "doing" and learned to "be." My mother—not the house—became the focus of my visits.

Making this transition wasn't easy at first. I carried with me years of resentment and anger: How many times in the past had my mother opted to clean the house over spending time with me? I asked myself: Why should I put chores aside for her now?

But I made an interesting discovery as I answered those questions: The past no longer existed for my mother. Alzheimer's had erased it. So what good would it do to revisit my childhood wounds at this juncture? It was not as if my mother could offer me any resolution of these issues now.

To meet my mother where she was, right then in the moment, I had to let go of the resentment I had harbored against her from childhood. To move forward with her. To be open to the gifts she had to offer me now. With each visit, I challenged myself to look inward at my own life. I repeatedly asked myself: Am I living with the same openness as she? With each answer, I brought myself closer to understanding my mother's world and my role in it.

In making a conscious choice to stop doing—to stop hiding behind the housework—I exposed myself to my mother in a new way. I felt unsafe and vulnerable at first. But then, as I grew more determined to be fully present for my mother, my compassion and understanding of her fears became absolute. I began to feel safer in the place of just "being" with her. I also began to feel better about the time we spent together. This new comfort level came by just allowing time to pass, time for each of us to become comfortable with a new habit of being with each other, and to relax into this new place, to trust it.

I was greatly rewarded for making this shift from *doing* to *being*. I discovered the richness of our interactions came from the quiet parts, the time we spent laughing or telling secrets, connecting with touch and eye contact, looking through family photos or a picture book, reading the love letters from the sailor she met when she was 16 years old, walking the neighborhood and petting the dogs. We learned to have fun together.

Somewhere along the way, my need to be *doing* just slipped away and was replaced by the joy and peace I felt just by *being* with her. I no longer approached my time with my mother as a set of tasks to be completed around the house or defined my value as what I could do to lighten everyone else's load. My value was in simply *being* with my mother.

The further along I traveled in changing my thinking, the less satisfied I was to stay locked away inside my childhood box of memories or to rely upon childlike views for interacting with my world. I welcomed the changes in me. This overwhelming desire for personal growth was another hidden gift of my mother's dementia.

Finally, as I shifted to recognize my own needs, I became an emotionally stronger companion to my mother. I found that I could carry a much heavier emotional load and continue walking effortlessly along beside her when I listened to my own inner truth. Learning to leave my agenda at home was a major success in this process.

It was now time to move forward and continue my companion journey of personal growth and transformation. This could only mean one thing: It was time for me to let go of the past and focus on the present with my mother.

Suggestions for Expressing and Recording Your Travels:

What is your agenda when you spend time with your loved one? Really analyze your motives and intentions, your needs and wants. Are you losing sight of your loved one? Who is in a better position to meet *both sets* of needs and wants?

_____

_____

_____

_____

_____

What must you do to "rightfully belong" on this journey with your loved one? For example, how was "love" defined in your family? What about "self-worth" and "value?" In what ways do you still carry these definitions of your self, and how do they prevent you from leaving your own agenda at home?

_____

_____

_____

_____

_____

What "props" do you hide behind when you relate to your loved one? Why do you think it is often scary to leave all of your props at home and come to be with your loved one as just yourself?

_____

_____

_____

_____

_____

Practical Suggestions to Help You Pave Your Path:

When you are spending time with your loved one, keep track of when and how your mind wanders. What other issues are bothering you? Are these issues within your control to change? If possible, make a list of these issues so that you can deal with them later and learn to refocus your attention on your loved one.

Contact a home-health agency to determine rates and services provided to assist with household chores, such as laundry, cleaning, etc. These agencies are listed in the phone book under "home health services" and you can also check with your local Chapter of the Alzheimer's Association for referrals.

Look for ways that you can blend your agenda with the former skills and interests of your loved one. Accomplish household chores together, if possible. This helps your loved one feel involved, helps them retain skills, and will help you connect with where your loved one is, mentally and physically.

TEN

Let Go of the Past

When we are mindful, deeply in touch with the present moment, our understanding of what is going on deepens, and we begin to be filled with acceptance, joy, peace and love.

THICH NHAT HANH

❀

My relationship with my mother had been tenuous from my earliest childhood. Apparently, I wanted more from her than she was able to give. That is, until she began her journey with dementia when she was 65 years old and I was 38 years old.

Dementia blew my relationship with my mother wide open. In the expansiveness created by this wake, many gifts flooded into my life, transforming my relationship with her, my family and myself and helping me to pave a path to peace through Alzheimer's.

One such gift was my mother's spontaneous expressions of love.

ALL YOU NEED IS LOVE

I was born in 1959, the last of four children who were all under the age of 10. My mother was a homemaker whose full-time job was to keep us clean, fed, and warm—visible displays of love and affection were not part of the "deal." My childhood memory was of a mother who was more interested in keeping her house clean than in spending time relating to her children. Our house was, for me, a cold and lonely place to grow up.

I don't recall my mother telling me as a child that I was loved and I don't remember getting hugs from her. Spontaneous expressions of love were simply not part of her personality—at least not then. It seemed easier for my mother to express affection toward her dogs than her own children. I grew up with this knowledge, and as an adult, I maintained a fairly passive relationship with my mother, born of duty more than delight.

With the onset of Alzheimer's, however, my mother became suddenly demonstrative and tender. This was one of many new dimensions of my mother's hard-wiring, evolving out of her demented mind.

Her kind and loving gestures often came out of the blue and without warning. Each time, they caught me off-guard. I had long ago given up hoping for this type of attention from my mother so when it finally came, it cut right to the heart of my very existence. This was the woman who made me and yet I hadn't known for sure until that moment that she loved me. Until then, she had not shared her feelings about me in a way that I could recognize as true.

The first time my mother told me how she felt about me, we were talking on the phone.

"I love you, Kathleen."

I didn't know what to do with the emotions those words set off inside me. Did my mother just tell me she loves me?

"Mom, I needed to hear those words from you when I was five!"

"Well, Kathleen, you're hearing them now."

A few months and many conversations later, my mother and I were walking my dog. We were laughing and enjoying the blowing leaves and warm autumn sunshine. At some point, my mother put her hand on my arm and we stopped. She looked directly at me and said:

"We love each other a lot, don't we?"

"Yes, we do, Mom. Every single day."

I then realized I no longer had any indignation or anger in my response. I felt no need to fight back, to discount her sentiment or to withhold my love from her. I had put down my weapons and defenses. I had turned inward, to the child-voice inside that told me it was finally time to trust my mother's expressions of love as sincere.

This voice, my intuition, knew what my consciousness had not yet absorbed—that I had become as open to receiving my mother's expressions of love as she had become in giving them to me. Our love finally had come together. Yes, maybe it was 40 years later than I had wanted, but it was just as rewarding.

What had changed in our relationship to alter my reaction to those words? My theory is that dementia changed the pattern of how my mother and I related to each other because it changed how we thought about each other. My mother had no choice in this transformation, but I did. And here is the gift: Our relationship changed precisely because I chose to accept my mother's dementia and to relate to her from a place of love, acceptance and peace.

A WORLD BEYOND TIME

Dementia remade my mother in two key ways. First, having Alzheimer's changed her job description and the focus of her daily life. There was no longer a time-clock in my mother's head and no longer a schedule of household duties to be completed every day. As my mother's world of *doing* became smaller and less familiar to her, her focus shifted. She was suddenly no longer interested in, or capable of, seeing life as a never-ending set of tasks to be completed on schedule. This had the effect of freeing her up, of giving her time to find new ways of expressing herself and connecting with the people around her.

Second, dementia had stripped away many of the negative elements of my mother's personality—the *hard-wiring* that had previously blocked our ability to connect. Like me, I suspect that my mother had her own childhood box filled with her own feelings that had kept her from living her life more fully. Dementia opened up my mother's box. She was no longer the distant and reserved parent I had known before this disease process overtook her brain. It was as if dementia had given my mother permission, along with a new set of skills, to be a different person in how she related to the people around her.

She became more loving and expressive. She was able to be tender with me and to nurture me, with facial expressions, words and touch. She developed the curiosity and openness of a child, allowing herself to be playful and to have fun. She let go of past judgments. She began to live in her emotions in the present. She became, in a sense, a blank slate.

Recognizing these "gifts" of her dementia, I made the commitment to let go of our past as well—to see my mother as she was in that moment, not as she had been when I was a child. The mother I had always known was no longer there—dementia had seen to that. What could I do to redefine how I thought about the person she had become?

I grew to understand that by keeping my feelings about her locked in the box labeled, "mother," I had also kept myself locked in a companion box—one that contained all of the murky memories and wounds that I ascribed to her from my childhood. As I spent time with my mother, I saw how dementia was opening her childhood box, releasing her. This challenged me to do the same—to let go of the many negative views of my mother that I had stored in my head for nearly 40 years. As I did, the barriers previously built up between us started to fade away.

LETTING GO OF ANGER

I became a true companion to my mother at the same time I transformed my wounded child. And in doing so, I was given the gift of releasing forever the anger I had held for so long.

Whatever negative emotions you may feel, whatever resentments or missed opportunities you have about your loved one, this journey demands you let go of them all. It is only when the barriers that separate you from your loved one fall that you can experience the transformative gifts Alzheimer's has to offer.

The process isn't always easy, however. When I first began spending Tuesday mornings with my mother, much of our time together was colored with my rage about how she had treated me as a child. The simplest activities with my mother could unexpectedly catapult me into a mood of reflection about my childhood with her.

For example, the first time I washed my mother's hair, I was unexpectedly transported back to my childhood. It is a humbling experience to cradle your mother's head in your hands. I could see how her hair had thinned with age, exposing patches of her pink scalp. The back of her neck was thin and lined with the crevices of age. Her head was heavy in my hands, reminding me of how fragile she was and how fragile I was, too.

I wondered if this was how I had looked and felt to her as a child when she cradled my head to wash my hair. I wondered if she had felt the same sort of tenderness and protectiveness for me in the moment of washing my hair as I felt for her now. The old me doubted that she had. I presumed she saw this ritual as just another chore to be completed on a never-ending schedule.

The rawness of this response overwhelmed me as it flashed across my thinking. My hands started to shake. I closed my eyes and tried to calm myself down to let this moment pass so I could finish washing my mother's hair. I felt guilty for having such thoughts and tried to push them from my mind. But, they lingered with me for some time.

The heaviness of my body on a particular day became a measure of my anger. Yet there I was, listening to her, caring for her, encouraging her and tending to her needs. Role reversals like this one continually exposed my buried childhood wounds—wounds that begged for resolution.

It is tempting to get stuck in the past—to hold onto the grudges and hurts from childhood. It is also easy to get bogged down by the irony of how you have become the parent to your parent. Examine these thoughts, but don't stay here. Move forward—grow up your child!

HEALING CHILDHOOD WOUNDS

My mother's dementia offered me a path out of this pattern of anger towards resolution of these childhood wounds. As my mother's personality crumbled away under the weight of dementia, my former distant and reserved mother was no longer present. She had vanished. In her place I found a newly vulnerable, confused, fearful, open woman, *a person in many respects just like me.* In the reflection of this new person, it seemed safe to finally discard my thinking about my former mother and to come into the present with this new one.

Each of us was opening our boxes, releasing those parts of ourselves propping up our traditionally strained relationship. We could come together in a new and loving relationship, if I would only choose to let go of the past and stay focused on the present moment with her. How could I do this?

With almost every other challenge on this journey, the key was in changing my thinking. Letting go of the past meant finding a way to think differently about my childhood. I could not change what happened to me as a child or how my mother had interacted with me. We both did the best we could do at the time. But that time in our history together was over. The power was in changing how I related to her in the present moment.

I recognized my mother's demented mind had no past frame of reference, and that she truly lived each moment of her life in the present moment. She was free in the present moment. Could I somehow choose to do the same thing? I asked myself several questions:

If the past no longer mattered to my mother, why did it matter so much to me?

What could I experience with her now if I just let it go?

And, more importantly:

Why I was so committed to retaining the pain, to holding

onto the past history with her, to maintaining my checklist of her "rights" and "wrongs?"

In other words: How did holding onto the past serve me?

By applying the thinking strategies outlined in Chapter 7, I came to understand how holding onto the past kept me distant from my mother. I could not feel "unloved" if I did not give my love to her. Thus, I had learned to keep myself separate from her as a survival tactic from childhood.

But now I realized that I no longer needed this protection. While it was important for me to honor the past and how I had survived my childhood, I could choose to live my life in the present differently with my mother. These realizations were the key to welcoming the possibility of reconnecting with her. With my load thus lightened, I was better able to walk alongside my mother and to more fully *embrace* her and her dementia. And, in this freer place, I began to transform my relationship with my mother and myself. At the foundation of this change was learning to reveal my true self.

Suggestions for Expressing and Recording Your Travels:

How has dementia changed your loved one's hard-wiring? Are they more loving? Combative? Belligerent? Can you separate the behavior from the person? Why or why not? Does the behavior remind you of someone else in your life?

_____

_____

_____

_____

_____

Think about your childhood box. What does it look like? What does it contain? What can you begin to let go of?

_____

_____

_____

_____

_____

Think about your loved one's childhood box. What might it contain? How might it be similar to yours? If you don't know, how can you begin a conversation about this topic? What are you willing to reveal about your own box?

_____

_____

_____

_____

_____

Practical Suggestions to Help You Pave Your Path:

If you are dealing with a parent-child relationship, know that you are now facing a time of shifting roles. Consider reading one of the many fine books on parent-child dynamics. See the "Additional Resources" section of this book for some suggestions.

Join a support group at your local Chapter of the Alzheimer's Association. The Association typically offers many types of specific groups, including groups for adult children, spouses, men, gays and lesbians, Spanish-speaking caregivers, etc.

Talk to your siblings about their past with your loved one. Do they have the same perspective? How is it different from yours? What can you learn from them?

ELEVEN

Reveal Your True Self

*There is a time for departure even
when there's no certain place to go.*

TENNESSEE WILLIAMS

❄

Up until my mother began her journey with dementia, I had been an expert at hiding my heart. My thoughts and feelings, my hopes and aspirations, often crushed as a child, were kept secret from her, locked safely inside my childhood box. We talked a lot about the weather in our adult relationship but never about the deep subjects of concern to either of us. It was just easier that way. Yet, it was on this part of our journey together that we each discovered the gift of sharing our true selves with each other.

Once Upon a Time

When I was five years old, we lived in North Denver, a neighborhood dotted with large shade trees and rich with ethnic diversity. I attended Beach Court Elementary School. With its green walls and high bright windows, Beach Court Elementary was a safe place for me to play and grow.

Kindergarten was all about playtime in 1964. Every school day was chock full of activity, including group games, story time, playing house, and my personal favorite, painting. The easels were set up in a corner of the room, the perfect spot to go if you were good at imagining far away places, as I was. I often spent my time wedged there, a smock transforming my clothes, to paint a picture. Each picture, painted with bright primary colors, contained roughly the same three elements: My house, my tree, my dog. My world.

I had a best friend, also named Kathleen. I remember attending a puppet show of "Hansel & Gretel" in the school auditorium with Kathleen and our mothers. The four of us sat together, Kathleen and me wedged between our mothers in the front row, holding hands and giggling ridiculously as only five-year old girls can do.

That day, I was wearing a brand new outfit: A pretty dress with a full, short skirt, patterned like a jumper on top. Beneath the skirt was my secret joy of that day: A pair of lacy white bloomers —the kind that fit over my plain, worn underwear, transforming them into something magical. I was so excited about showing my new bloomers to Kathleen that I stood up, lifted the corners of my skirt and twirled round and round so my friend could see my lacy secret, from every angle.

That moment of pure and innocent expression ended abruptly when my mother grabbed me, yanking my skirt back into place. Covered up. Hushed. Safe.

My mother scowled at me and through gritted teeth, admonished me about my unladylike behavior: *You are never to do that again, do you hear me? You just don't know how to behave in public, do you? Wait until we get home, young lady.*

My mother's face flushed red in embarrassment over my "indiscretion." I had humiliated myself in front of everyone there. Oh, the unbearable horror of it all for my mother! But, I was only five—I had no armor for this battle. Yet.

My exuberance deflated instantly, crushed by the weight of my own shame and anger. The puppet show commenced, the scenes played out, the show ended. I missed most of it, lost in my own thoughts, comparing my mother to the witch in the story.

As I look back on this experience, I wonder how my mother could have thought that a five-year old was capable of indiscretion or how my actions could have been interpreted as anything but innocent excitement. What I now realize is that it was the display of my body that so upset her and drove her to act quickly and without compassion. She expected me to be as modest as she was.

Something shut down in me that day, some little piece of innocent joy and worthiness withered up and died. This was the beginning of my habit of hiding myself and of retreating into my childhood box. There would be many more opportunities to replay this scene, continuing well into my adulthood.

But then along came dementia, changing everything between us. When dementia altered my mother's hard-wiring, my aloof and critical parent was no longer present. In response to my mother's new personality, it no longer made sense for me to continue hiding myself from her. And so, I embarked upon a path of self-disclosure.

REBUILDING TRUST, ONE STORY AT A TIME

Starting small at first, I began to reveal tiny personal details of my work life and my relationships to my mother. Nothing too emotionally charged for me, just so I didn't risk her disapproval or criticism. But neither happened. Instead, my disclosures were met with genuine warmth and acceptance. Over and over I tested this new way of relating, each time revealing just a little bit more. Each time, my mother responded similarly. Sometimes she even initiated the conversation by asking questions about my life or by revealing her personal thoughts, such as her belief that everyone deserved to have someone to love in life.

In the beginning, her self-disclosures were as tentative as mine—I think my mother also was testing me. Perhaps somewhere inside her tangled thinking, she likewise feared my dismissal or criticism, knowing I could only give to her what I had received from her.

Slowly, in the midst of these honest conversations, my child self began to emerge from hiding, transforming my relationships with myself and with my mother. As I grew more confident, I learned how to better hear my inner voice and to find ways for my child to speak directly to my mother's child. And she reciprocated. We played, we laughed until we cried, or we just cried. Most importantly, we connected. My adult-self transformed in the process. I now saw my mother as just another person, just another soul seeking understanding.

It was then that my childlike views of her finally grew up. I came to understand that, in raising me, she did the best she could, and more than this, she parented me most likely in the manner she herself had been parented. She could not give to me what she had not received from her own parents. I released my mother from the anchor of my blame.

Rediscovering Joy

Months passed and my critical and dismissing adult-self began to trust these new ways of relating were genuine. As a result, I let go of the idea that hiding myself was the only way to survive in rela-

A person with dementia whose mental abilities are declining is likely to feel vulnerable and in need of reassurance and support. It is important that you do everything you can to help them retain their sense of identity and their feelings of self worth. The Alzheimer's Association suggests learning the life story of your loved one, so that you can see the whole person, rather than simply the person with dementia.

tionship with my mother. In fact, I came to the opposite conclusion. My adult-self came to trust that only by revealing my true self could I fully embrace this journey with her.

The pieces of myself that had been left shut down and dying that day so long ago at Beach Court Elementary came back to life as I regularly interacted with my mother. I rediscovered the joy of my five-year old self, and my sense of inherent worthiness strengthened. I found out that a self without the walls of a box around me was a more positive place to live my life and a stronger path upon which to accompany my mother on her journey with dementia.

My mother's box seemed to open as well, although perhaps not so purposefully as mine. As she slowly returned to her essential self, without the walls of her former personality boxing her in, she began to share parts of herself and her thinking previously unknown to me. In doing so, she became more vulnerable, like me. Dementia single-handedly freed up my mother to be more loving and expressive, more tender and nurturing, more fun-loving and curious. She lived in her emotions for perhaps the very first time in her life, and I believe this gave her a sense of personal freedom and empowerment. Most importantly, she no longer held herself separate from me. She *embraced* me.

As this opening happened for both of us, the barriers between us and the need for separateness, both in place since my early childhood, fell away. We were able to finally embrace each other in a new positive and healthy way. With each gift I discovered, my mother and I drew closer, until my path to peace became *our path of peace.*

I liked this place. I began to pay closer attention to my mother. What else did she have to share with me? And, would we have enough time to find it?

Suggestions for Expressing and Recording Your Travels:

Identify a pivotal moment in your life defining your parent-child relationship—it may be an embarrassing moment, a childhood wound, or an unforgiven slight. How does this moment still define your relationship?

_____

_____

_____

_____

_____

Dementia may have erased your loved one's memories of the past—the same memories that you still carry around with you and which may negatively affect your relationship. In what ways do you hide your true self from your loved one and why? What will it take for you to put down your load of past memories, and begin new, fresh, today?

_____

_____

_____

_____

It is very tempting to get bogged down by your childlike views of your parent—what childlike views do you have? How do these views play out in other relationships? Pick one, and grow it up!

_____

_____

_____

_____

_____

Practical Suggestions to Help You Pave Your Path:

Make a list of five things you want to share with your loved one. These items could be childhood wounds, secrets, joys, or concerns. Visualize talking with your loved one about these items and see a positive outcome. Then, pick one topic and start the conversation.

Be attentive to your self-talk. Look for critical thoughts of yourself and your loved one. Revisit your dictionary of life and begin to rework your thoughts using the steps outlined in Chapter 7.

Be gentle with yourself. The revelations you will discover along this part of the path may become overwhelming. Take whatever time you need to process this new information.

TWELVE

Pay Attention to Your Loved One as if She is a Prophet

I am beginning to learn that it is the sweet, simple things of life which are the real ones after all.

LAURA INGALLS WILDER

❀

Some people believe dementia represents a loss of the self. Not me. I believe dementia is one pathway for returning to the essential self. It is a place of unconditional love and acceptance, where the soul is freed from the earthly tethers of personality and ego.

Unencumbered by reality, by absolutes in thinking, the demented mind knows no boundaries. Certainly, a demented person's behavior can often be childlike, but sometimes the displays of raw emotion and the words coming out of my mother's mouth were full of wisdom. The more I emptied myself of the guilt and blame of my childhood box, the easier it was for me to see the opportunity before me.

And so I began to pay attention to my mother as if she were

a prophet. It was along this part of the path I received the gift of unconditional love from my mother.

In this demented land, my mother lived in her emotions. She smiled, she became angry or agitated, she wrung her hands, she sighed, she looked away and she laughed with her whole body. Words were not important: She simply emoted. She didn't explain why she did these things. As I adjusted my expectations of her, I no longer looked for an explanation, relying instead upon the wisdom of my child-self to interpret my mother's behavior. This was another way I reconnected with my mother and myself on this journey.

When my mother's words were no longer clear, I looked to her behavior as a communication tool. Very often, her body language told the story loud and clear. I didn't need my mother to tell me she was afraid of the doctor. I just had to watch her wring her hands or hear her sighs to know the turmoil going on inside her.

IT WAS ALL IN HER EYES

I learned to pay attention to everything about my mother—her words, her emotions, the movements of her body and, most importantly, to the expressions of her face, especially her eyes. Brown in color, the emotional honesty they conveyed was sometimes overwhelming to me. My mother's eyes said it all—they could flash anger, pour forth love and understanding, light up with humor, dull with fear, or swell up red and instantly fill with tears. They were truly a window to her soul, and it was by paying attention to her eyes that I truly felt her unconditional love for me for the first time in my life.

It happened one day when my mother and I went to a fast-food restaurant for lunch. Usually, we would purchase our meals and then drive home to eat, but on this day it was very quiet in the

As you're becoming increasingly attuned to Mom's nonverbal communication, a private language may develop between the two of you. The unexpected bonus of caring for an Alzheimer's person is that, often, you feel closer to that person while learning to interpret the subtle signs of nonverbal communication.

JYTTE LOKVIK, MA
Alzheimer's A to Z, Quick Reference Guide

restaurant, and so we decided to take our lunch in one of the booths. There was an older man washing the windows and wiping off the tables. My mother seemed to enjoy watching him at his work, the repetitive circular motions of his arms probably soothing to her. I was sitting across from her, two feet between us.

"I have been thinking a lot about death lately, Kathleen."

She fixed her brown eyes on me and waited for my response.

"Mom, I'm not ready for you to die yet. This time we spend together is so good for me."

As I choked on my food, my mother continued to stare at me. The honesty conveyed by her focused gaze was too much for me to bear. There was something different about her eyes—something I had never seen before, something I was not sure I recognized, but desperately hoped could be true. *Could this be what love looked like?*

As I began to cry, my mother's eyes also welled up with tears. *"It is for me, too. But, I'm ready to go, you know?"*

"Yes, I know, Mom."

I could imagine how my mother might have grown tired of trying to make it right with herself, tired of trying to hide the declining parts of her body and mind. Unlike me, she could not see how dementia was opening her box, loosening up her formerly hard-wired personality. Perhaps she only knew she was perpetually confused and angry, out of control. Perhaps she wondered where God was, the God she had prayed to her entire life. Perhaps, she wondered why this was happening to her. If so, all this wondering had left her exhausted. And her eyes said it all, and more.

If I had not been sitting across from my mother, just two feet separating us, paying attention to the totality of her physical being, I would have missed all that she had tried to convey to me that day. I would have missed the first time I had seen her looking at me with unconditional love and acceptance. I would have missed seeing her truth and the feeling of my heart expanding and contracting almost simultaneously, opening to capture the moment, then closing to be sure I held it inside forever. I would have missed our spirits linking as we talked about love, death, and loss.

THE SOUND OF TRUTH

Just as I learned to look more closely, I also began to listen with sharper ears and an open heart to what my mother was saying. Sometimes hidden in my mother's jumbled words was a pearl of truth or wisdom, a before-unspoken observation about humanity or relationships that was often like a very fine laser aimed precisely at healing the receiver. It was easy to get into the habit of dismissing what she said as nonsense, and in the beginning, I was guilty of doing this. But as I quieted my mind and nurtured my inner voice, as I unloaded my own emotional issues and broke down the walls of my childhood box, my heart began to hear the hidden meanings she was conveying to me.

"*I love you.*"

She would say those words not just to convey affection, but also at moments when I was experiencing a bout of built-up anxiety, frustration or anger in a particular situation.

"*I love you.*"

Those words became a mantra for my mother. Perhaps they were her way of explaining her inability to control her behavior or to follow my instructions or to say she was sorry.

Watching her do this, and realizing what a calming effect it had on me, I began to use this same technique with her. And it worked.

When she was being particularly difficult, "*I love you.*"

When she no longer recognized me and could no longer speak, "*I love you.*"

The words acted like a brick that wedged open the rational door of my mother's brain, making reasoning with her, connecting with her, possible for just a single moment. Sometimes this was all it took to calm down the situation for both of us.

LISTENING WITH MY HEART

Paying attention to my mother as if she was a prophet enabled me to capture these rare and unpredictable insights from her behavior and her words. I felt challenged to reciprocate with an insight of my own, to look at my own thinking and behavior to determine if I was living my life with the same openness as she was. This helped me to find new ways for adjusting my expectations of her, for letting go of past hurts and for accepting her offerings as the truth for her now. In other words, paying attention illuminated many gifts, allowing me to transform myself in relation to her.

If I had not been diligent in paying close attention to her, it would have been easy for me to miss her efforts to reconnect with me and to stay stuck in my childhood box, recycling my old negative thinking about our relationship. By staying open and alert to the messages my mother had to offer, I remained positive and strong as I traveled along beside her. But the full value of those messages did not become clear until I began to express and record them as part of my travels with my mother.

The Alzheimer's Society has the following recommendations to help you focus on your loved one's remaining abilities:

- Give them plenty of encouragement. Let them do things at their own pace and in their own way.
- Do things with the person, rather than for them, so that they can preserve some independence.
- Break activities down into small steps so that they feel a sense of achievement, even if they can only manage a part of a task.

Suggestions for Expressing and Recording Your Travels:

What are the obstacles that prevent you from hearing what your loved one is saying? What clues can you find in your loved one's behavior? Can you begin to look beyond the spoken words, or into the silence of no words and let your intuition hear what your loved one is saying?

_____

_____

_____

_____

_____

It has been said that we often give what we want in return. What words and actions soothed you as a child? How can you share these with your loved one? In sharing, do you find that you also are soothed?

_____

_____

_____

_____

_____

I believe that dementia may be one path to returning to the essential self—the shedding of reality. Can you see any signs of this in your loved one? How can you take this lesson into your daily life?

_____

_____

_____

_____

_____

Practical Suggestions to Help You Pave Your Path:

There are several great books with common sense approaches to interacting with a person with dementia. I particularly appreciated *Dancing on Quicksand, A Gift of Friendship in the Age of Alzheimer's* by Marilyn Mitchell. See the "Additional Resources" section of this book for this and other reading options.

As you navigate the emotional terrain of this journey, remember that you can reach out and share your experience with a support group or call the 24-hour toll-free support line courtesy of your local Chapter of the Alzheimer's Association.

Slow down and listen to what your heart is saying. Welcome each change of emotion. Ask for guidance. Trust that you know what is right for you. Keep a journal!

THIRTEEN

Express and Record Your Travels

The only real voyage of discovery consists not in seeking new landscapes but in having new eyes.

MARCEL PROUST

❁

My steady companions on this journey with my mother were the various ways I expressed and recorded my travels with her. This step empowered me to stay the course and enabled me to see the personal growth and transformation that resulted as I accompanied my mother on her journey. Keeping track of my thoughts and feelings also helped me to clear away much of the debris that sometimes blocked our travels together.

Hidden under this debris, I eventually found my true voice, my child's voice that lived deeply down inside of me. I nurtured and honored that discovery, tapping into the strength and guidance of my inner voice along this path. When all else failed me, my voice frequently guided me on how to interact with my mother.

Finally, by actively processing my journey, I became free to stay in the moment with my mother, trusting that my processing of what was happening was right for me, relieved of the burden to keep everything locked in my head.

J ust as you have the need to embrace your travels, so does your loved one. Just like you, a person with dementia will also experience a range of emotions during the journey through Alzheimer's. Your loved one has the right to expect those caring for her to listen and to try to understand how she feels, offering support, rather than ignoring or minimizing her experience.

A Legacy of This Journey

As discussed in Chapter 7, one method of recording my travels was the ongoing process of editing my "dictionary of life," reworking the definitions I had of myself, my world, my roles and relationships with myself, my mother, other family members. Each time I "felt bad" on my journey, I sought refuge in this process. It enabled me to clearly map out my path with my mother, using *my own* definitions, instead of someone else's. Editing my dictionary was a very powerful tool, helping me to remove blame from my life and to take responsibility for where I found myself, in my *entire* life, not just my life with a terminally ill mother.

Another method of expressing and recording my travels with my mother was to write stories about my past and recent interactions with her, often painfully dredging through the memories from my childhood and my more recent experiences with her dementia. Writing stories helped me to work through many of the "glitches" in my thinking about my wounded childhood and to make new memories of my mother. Putting my stories onto paper released me; I no longer had to carry them with me on this journey. Many of these stories captured how my mother's personality changed along her path with dementia. To the extent I still live inside my childhood box, it is lined with these new and positive images of my mother. In this way, I continue to hold my mother inside of me now that she is no longer on this earth.

I have shared my travels with others by writing this book, speaking to groups, and conducting workshops for caregivers about the power of the journey through Alzheimer's. I have shared my stories with friends facing dementia in their families and brought the skills I have learned into my Elder Law practice with my clients. I have learned much from observing and hearing about the journeys of others with their loved ones and of the ways they have come to embrace the dementia of their spouses, siblings, and parents.

All of these ways of expressing and recording my travels helped me to process this amazing journey with my mother and to incorporate what I have learned into the other areas of my life. Sometimes, these connections will not be immediately clear, and so preserving your thoughts for later reflection is invaluable. Writing also can be a way to highlight those situations in the rest of your life where you may need to consider taking more responsibility for where you find yourself. Finally, keeping a record of your travels will also help you to bring closure to this experience at the end of your journey.

Recording and expressing your travels with your loved one can be a powerful way to understand your own thoughts and feelings, and to uncover the strength and resolve to remain a strong companion on this difficult path. By keeping a record of your experiences, you can begin to connect the dots between your thinking and the outcomes of your entire life. Start with the suggestions at the end of each Chapter. Then, I encourage you to use your own expressiveness to look for ways not only to improve your own life but the lives of your family and friends also dealing with dementia.

Suggestions for Expressing and Recording Your Travels:

Spend five minutes after each interaction with your loved one to capture your thoughts and feelings about your journey. In the car, back at the office, before bed—get in the habit of writing it down for later reflection.

_____

_____

_____

_____

_____

How have you experienced your new "dictionary of life" in your life? What seems to be working better? What feelings have changed? Is caregiving easier?

_____

_____

_____

_____

_____

What are some ways of incorporating your new thinking in ALL areas of your life?

_____

_____

_____

_____

_____

Practical Suggestions to Help You Pave Your Path:

Recognize that there will never be another experience like this journey. Decide early on how to record your travels. Do you prefer to keep a handwritten journal? A computer journal? Pick a method that is consistent with your preferences and lifestyle.

Listen more closely to friends and colleagues about their experiences with dementia. Compare to your own experiences and celebrate your victories, however small!

Make a list of three ways you can share your wisdom about embracing dementia with others. Then, do it!

FOURTEEN

One Last Story— Pulling It All Together

And now here is my secret, a very simple secret; it is only with the heart that one can see rightly, what is essential is invisible to the eye.

ANTOINE DE SAINT-EXUPERY

❀

It is tempting to focus on what is lost throughout the progression of dementia. As my mother's dementia advanced, she lost much of the "hard-wiring" of her personality. Yet, this ultimately became a blessing that made possible the transformation of our relationship. Still, my mother also lost many of her skills and hobbies and, with these, much of the joy of her life.

Losses experienced on the journey of dementia come in many forms and may include the loss of shared memories, predictable responses, peace of mind and hope, personal freedom, family stability, shared love and companionship, and personal identity as important relationships shift and adapt to this disease process.

The list of losses is seemingly endless. But the list of its potential gifts can be equally long—it simply depends on how you choose to view this journey.

In my experience, the losses experienced as a result of Alzheimer's often highlighted a previously hidden gift or a forgotten memory. It was at these moments I found unexpected joy and richness as I traveled the path with my mother. As I learned to shift my focus from the inevitable losses of Alzheimer's to the gifts that waited for me along the way, I tapped into unending reserves of strength and compassion that guided me as I accompanied my mother to the end of her journey.

One such forgotten memory was also one of the most cherished memories I had of my mother's participation in my childhood. It was about books and our shared love of reading. I have a vivid picture in my head of my mother, curled up in her favorite chair in the family room every afternoon before dinner in what I called her "do not disturb position," immersed in one of her beloved mystery novels. Reading was her most-cherished and only leisure activity—and it is one of the great loves she passed along to me (along with her passion for classical music and dogs).

My mother took me to the library every week to pick out new books. She would enter me in the library's summer reading contest each year and, by August, I would come home with a ribbon of achievement. I racked up many such awards over my childhood and they were a source of my self esteem. To this day, I am proud of my reading and writing abilities, and I know I have my mother to thank for these skills.

Unfortunately, as my mother's dementia progressed, she lost her ability to read. She no longer recognized most words or had the ability to keep track of the story. But, she still seemed to retain her love of reading. We spent many contented hours huddled together on the couch looking at picture books and I often read to her from her prayer book or a magazine.

A Turning Point in Our Journey

One Tuesday, when I was visiting, she said she had something she wanted to show me. I was excited because it was rare when my mother could remember a thought long enough to share it with anyone. What she wanted to share with me was an essay in a book, titled *"Eulogy of the Dog,"* by George G. Vest.[10] She wanted to read this short piece to me. So, we sat down at the kitchen table and she started to read. Well, sort of.

My mother actually could read only about one out of every three words—the other two were a jumble of letters and sounds. She combined the words together and often reversed their order. She began to read faster and faster, as if her mind were telling her to speed up and get through it. Her voice was flat and her speech was slurred. I was horrified. When had my mother lost her ability to read?

I became frantic. I desperately wanted to give her back what Alzheimer's had cruelly stolen.

"Mom, the word is jury, not oggi."

"Mom, you missed a sentence here."

"Mom, let's start again."

"Mom!!!"

But here's the thing: My mother appeared to have no idea she couldn't read. She was just going along, joyfully sharing this story with me, just like I imagine she did when I was a child. The difference was when I was a child, it was *me* who saw a jumble of words on the page and it was *my* mind that sped ahead, trying to catch on to what she was saying—yet another role reversal on this journey with my mother.

What my mother did know was that I was becoming more and more anxious. Like many Alzheimer's patients who lose the benefit of everyday language, my mother had grown more perceptive of those around her.

Clearly, I needed to calm down. I saw how my panic was washing over my mother. And no amount of correcting her was going to change the fact: Alzheimer's had erased my mother's ability to recognize words.

This was a moment of choice. Would I let my anxiety ruin our time together? Or could I find another way to view this loss?

I managed a smile, *"Go on, Mom. Keep reading."*

As she turned back to the story, my choice was made. Something changed in me. I no longer noticed her stumbles. I heard only the love song that had been there all along. My mother was reading to me from her heart, perhaps from that very place that still remembered our weekly trips to the library together. Alzheimer's couldn't take that away from us.

Here is how the change occurred. Listening to my mother, I was once again reminded of the devastating effects of dementia, of how much my mother gave up each day to this disease. I realized my mother had most likely lost her ability to read forever. Something she had enjoyed for more than 60 years had just been erased from her life. This joyful piece of her life was gone.

I was filled with grief and anger over all that dementia had stolen from her. Acting out of this hurtful place, I had tried to correct her misspoken words, to teach her how to read again. I interrupted her, rereading the sentences and trying to clarify the meaning of the words for her. We had to get it right. It was so important to get it right! After all, reading was all about recognizing the words and understanding their meaning.

But, as I did this, my mother just looked at me with a confused, hurt look, and kept on reading in her own style and at her own pace. And when she finished, she was obviously pleased with herself for sharing the story with me, much like I had been when, as a child, I had stumbled through reading a story to her.

My mother did not realize she had made no sense at all. That is, unless I chose to tell her. I made the choice to remain quiet. More than this, I made the choice to stop correcting her in this context and otherwise.

If I was going to make it through to the end of this journey with my mother—if I wanted to be in as healthy and peaceful a place as possible in the face of her decline and eventual death—I needed to embrace the moment with her and meet her where she was each time I saw her. I also had to adjust my expectations of her. And in order to be authentic in these endeavors, I made the conscious choice to change my thinking about this loss of her and to consider instead if there was a way to *think* of this as a gift.

A Gift of the Heart

As I made this shift in my thinking, in the moment of sitting next to her at the kitchen table, I was reminded of how it was my mother who had given me the gift of reading in the first place. She had made reading a priority in my life. This was perhaps the only part of her she freely shared with me as a child. Reading was the legacy she had given me.

Reading opened up new worlds to me and comforted me in the loneliness of my childhood. Books were my companions and my teachers, my friends and my therapists. I hid behind books when I had no words or means to express my emotions. I traveled to far away places and tried new things with each book I read. Likewise, a trip to the library was a trip into wonderland. I would never come home with fewer than three new books in my hands, held close to my chest like treasured possessions.

Reading continues to play a major role in my adult life. It is the way I relax at the end of the day, the way I solve problems, and the way I learn more about myself and my world. And to this day, I prefer to get my books at the library. I am not a book-buyer. When I walk into a library, I still feel this expansiveness in my chest, like anything is possible and everything exists within these walls. I just have to find it!

What a powerful belief to have in my life. Each time I go in search of new books to read, I am reminded it was my mother who gave me this lifetime gift. And I still check-out no fewer than three new books with each visit, greedily clutching them to my chest and hurrying home to open them up and begin a new adventure.

These cherished memories of my childhood and the continuing role reading has played in my adult life, filled me with overwhelming joy and warmth about reading as I sat with my mother that day. I had shifted my consciousness from my mother's loss to my gain. It was true that my mother had lost her ability to read and this saddened me terribly. But within me, forever, were the gifts of being able to read and the love of libraries I received from her. Alzheimer's could not take these gifts away from me!

A Catalyst for Change

Choosing to stay in the present moment with my mother that day, to welcome the pain and devastation of the moment, and to practice shifting my thinking from negative thoughts about her losses to positive thoughts about the gifts of traveling this path with her, was one way dementia became a catalyst for positive change within myself. I now had the skills and courage to apply this process to all the difficult moments of my life, and to let go of her when the time came.

Marilyn Mitchell, author of *Dancing on Quicksand, A Gift of Friendship in the Age of Alzheimer's*,[11] offers several practical tips for accompanying a person with dementia, including:

- About the "truth"—in public when necessary, spare your loved one and others the embarrassment of absolute truthfulness; in private, patiently and lovingly tell your loved one even the hardest truths.

- When you find yourself in the "loop"—the obsessive spinning circles of your loved one's mind—simply change the subject of your conversation.

- Repeatedly using your loved one's name will ground her in the present and remind her that the two of you are connected.

Suggestions for Expressing and Recording Your Travels

Make a list of all of the "losses" you have experienced with your loved one's dementia. Then, take each "loss" and see how you can rethink it into a neutral event, or better yet, a positive one. Leave no stone unturned. Go back to your childhood and work your way through your other relationships. Explore your thinking.

_____

_____

_____

_____

_____

Write a story about your parent or loved one—before dementia. Something that makes you feel good. You can return to that story later, on days when you are feeling bad.

_____

_____

_____

_____

_____

Capture the positive memories you have of your loved one—from the past, and from this day forward. Write these memories down. When you are feeling bad, reread one of those memories and see if you can turn "feeling bad" into a new insight or plan of action.

Practical Suggestions to Help You Pave Your Path:

Reading is a part of the legacy my mother left with me. What is the legacy you received from your loved one?

Think about how you will feel at the death of your loved one. Then imagine how you would like to feel. Begin now to lay the foundation for your imagination. For example, I wanted to feel joy when my mother died, and I did. This was because I had done my work with her before she died and I had internalized what I learned from her. I owned her love for me and death could not take this away from me. I still have those feelings of love with me now.

FIFTEEN

Mom, Are You There?

There are four kinds of people in the world: Those who have been caregivers, those who currently are caregivers, those who will be caregivers, and those who will need caregivers.

ROSALYNN CARTER
Former First Lady

❀

I'll never forget the day when my mother no longer recognized me. I knew then that at some point in the not-so-distant future, my mother would cease to exist. It was tempting to focus on this and other losses. But even as I watched Alzheimer's chip away at my mother's mind and body, I was in awe of the gifts left behind.

Alzheimer's forever transformed the landscape of our relationship. Along this journey, my mother and I drew closer than at any other point in our lives. My mother lived completely in the moment. Without history to claim her attention, she was totally present; childlike, even. And I learned to take her hand as we walked across the street together.

We lived in the twilight, that 'tween time of uncertainty. Physically, my mother was there. Mentally, she was more often not. But, each day, she gave me incredible gifts.

As a companion to my mother through Alzheimer's, I learned to embrace and love the child within myself.

❀

As I walked alongside my mother, I identified and then shed many of the contents of my childhood box which had previously kept me locked me away from my life and my mother. I could now more fully connect with my world.

❀

I reconnected with my child-self and found my true voice and truth in the process. Speaking from a place of intuition and openness, I was able to become an advocate for my mother and to express myself more freely along this journey. This intuitive presence helped me to understand my mother's behaviors and emotions when words failed her. In the process, I recaptured the joy I had felt as a child.

❀

I developed new definitions of myself, my worth, and my role on this journey. I let go of my need to be doing, and became comfortable just being with my mother. Editing my "dictionary of life" gave me tools that were more adaptive and supportive of me in my entire life.

❀

I relearned trust, finally knowing that I did not need to stay quiet and invisible, inside my childhood box, to survive. I stepped forward along this journey and, as a result, thrived with my mother and my family.

❀

I finally released the weight of anger I had long carried against my mother. When I did this, I grew up my child's relationship with my mother and began to see her through the eyes of an adult. I felt much lighter and healthier after this release. It was much easier to connect with my mother without this weight wedged between us.

❀

I healed many of the childhood wounds I ascribed to my mother. I let them go forever, releasing the guilt and blame that had tainted my relationships with my mother and myself. This helped me to meet my mother, heart-to-heart and soul-to-soul, in the present moment of her life.

❀

I learned to take responsibility for my life by reinforcing my understanding of the connection that exists between thoughts, feelings, and outcomes. In so doing, I kept the power inside of me, never letting it go to the situation or to another person.

❀

And finally, I became a more understanding, patient, and compassionate Elder Law attorney as I worked through issues with my family that led to healthier ways of communicating with my clients.

❀

Each of these breakthroughs helped me to transform my relationship with my mother. At the beginning of this journey, we were like strangers. Over time, and as I found my path to peace, our relationship grew deeper and more loving.

One Tuesday my mother and I spent our time together running errands. We started off with a haircut for her, with a new beautician. It did not go very well as the beautician treated my mother as if she were a child, calling her "honey" throughout the wash and cut. We laughed about it all morning. After the hair cut, we went to a store to buy her some clothes. This was always a challenge because she could not easily figure out how to take off her existing clothes to try on new ones, and she was so modest she did not want my help. Next, we did some shopping I needed to do, and we finished up with lunch at our favorite fast-food restaurant, Arby's. On the way home, we stopped to watch some llamas owned by a family up the street and to feed a neighborhood dog named "Bear."

"Boy, we did a lot today, didn't we? What was your favorite part, Mom?"

"You."

Wow, need I say more? And the personal growth did not stop there.

By embracing my mother's dementia, our relationship grew and deepened in many ways.

❀

I began to see my mother more clearly. I decided she had her own childhood box, filled with many of the same contents as mine. As she revealed herself, emptying her box of its contents, I reciprocated. This created a new heart bond between us.

❀

By changing my definition of "mother," I came to see she was just another human being, like me. I could now find new ways to connect with her by drawing on the similar parts of each of us.

❀

I made new and healthy memories of my mother, to replace the negative childhood memories I carried with me as an adult; these new memories give me comfort and support me now that my mother is gone.

❀

I learned by giving my full attention to her prophesies, I gained many helpful insights about myself and where I came from.

❀

I embraced her spontaneous expressions of love for me. I came to believe these expressions were her truth, and honored and accepted them into my heart. I came to truly love my mother with every fiber of my being.

❀

I became an advocate for my mother—standing up to her and for her on this journey. I stepped out of my childhood box and took up a new position within my family. I spoke my mind and I survived!

❀

And finally, as a result of my mother's Alzheimer's, the door was opened for me to transform my relationships with my family.

❀

I developed new techniques for communicating with my father, allowing me to work with him—adult to adult—for the benefit of my mother.

❀

I encouraged and supported my sister's journey with our mother, a journey much different than mine. Along the way, we found new common ground to bring our love of our mother and of each other together.

❀

I asserted my value as the "objective" Elder Law attorney guiding my family along this treacherous path.

❀

I shed "the kid" and "little sister" personas.

❀

Alzheimer's changed not just my mother's life. It changed everything. Out of so much loss came a road map for loving my mother, loving myself, and for living my life with greater patience and purpose. *This is what I mean when I say I found a path to peace through Alzheimer's.* You can find your own path, too. Learn to welcome the chaos swirling inside. Then, remember the three basic questions that can bring you peace:

1. **"Who can I turn to for information and support?"** will lead you to specialists who can help you make the right choices;

2. **"How do I prepare myself for this journey?"** will take you inward to discover what *you* think and feel about Alzheimer's; and

3. **"How can I stay open to the gifts this experience has to offer?"** will help bring you personal growth and transformation.

When my mother was diagnosed, I saw two paths ahead: The first one was sad and familiar; the second one, new and full of possibility. I chose to take the path to peace through Alzheimer's and it made all the difference for my mother—and for me. Without the onset of my mother's dementia and the impact it had on me and my family, I might not have embraced this journey to transform myself and my relationships with others. I might have stayed in my childhood box forever. And I would have missed much of what life has to offer.

Recognizing this, I can honestly say that I am grateful for my mother's dementia. It is perhaps the greatest gift she ever gave to me.

As my mother slipped further into dementia, and even when she finally let go of this world, I didn't have to ask: Mom, are you there? I already knew that wherever she was in her journey, we were there together.

Suggestions for Expressing and Recording Your Travels:

Make a list of all the gifts you have received, and the personal transformations you have experienced, on your journey through Alzheimer's. Now, celebrate!

_____

_____

_____

_____

_____

_____

_____

_____

_____

_____

_____

_____

EPILOGUE

*There are only two ways to live
your life. One is as though nothing
is a miracle. The other is as though
everything is a miracle.*

ALBERT EINSTEIN

❀

EULOGY FOR A MOTHER

April 5, 1931 to July 17, 2004

There are certain things that will forever remind me of my mother.

Take petunias, for example. My mother had a love/hate relationship with petunias. She felt they did not bloom enough... Maybe because she routinely picked the blooms off thinking they were already dead.

My mother had an irrational love affair with street cleaners. She would stop the car to watch them go by; come out of the house to watch them go by. Maybe it was the combination of their goliath size and their graceful movement.

My mother was known for her deep, sudden, uncontrollable, all-consuming blushes.

Then, there was her habit of washing the tops of cans before she opened them. This mystified me, until one day I asked her why she did it. She said, because they're … DIRTY.

Which brings me to her favorite perfume: Clorox.

My mother was a product of her time. Her friend, Georgia Liley, told me that mothering in the 50's was a job, complete with a time clock, a set of tasks to complete every day, and a performance review.

My mother was an exemplary worker. She kept us kids and the house clean. She kept us fed. She insisted I wear rubber boots in wet weather.

But, she rarely showed affection for us. You know the kind of affection that both squeezes the life out of you and fills you up at the same time?

And then, along came Alzheimer's and it changed everything.

Over the last few years, she couldn't tell you often enough how much she loved you.

She couldn't hug you, touch you, smile at you or kiss you often enough to show you how much she loved you.

What a gift!

I spent almost every Tuesday morning with my mother for the last three years. We found many things to do together, like:

- Reading old love letters from the sailor she met when she was 16 years old. Talk about blushing.

- Endlessly flipping through a book of Norman Rockwell paintings, searching for the splash of red or the dog.

- Trolling the neighborhood for dogs to pet and feed, my mother bending over the fence with no fear, just love.

- Reading and rereading her favorite story, called *Eulogy of the Dog*. I would like to share that story with you now:

Gentlemen of the jury, the best friend man has in the world may turn against him and become his worst enemy. His son or daughter whom he has reared with loving care may prove ungrateful. Those who are nearest and dearest to us—those whom we trust with our happiness and good name—may become traitors to their faith. The money a man has he may lose. It flies away from him, perhaps when he needs it most. A man's reputation may be sacrificed in a moment of ill-considered action. The people who are prone to fall on their knees to do us honor when success is with us may be the first to throw the stone of malice when failure settles its clouds upon our head. The one absolutely unselfish friend that man can have in this selfish world—the one that never deserts him, the one that never proves ungrateful or treacherous—is his dog.

Gentlemen of the jury, a man's dog stands by him in prosperity and poverty, in health and in sickness. He will sleep on the cold ground when the wintry winds blow and the snow drives fiercely, if only to be near his master's side. He will kiss the hand that has no food to offer, he will lick the wounds and sores that come in encounter with the roughness of the world. He guards the sleep of his pauper master as if he were a prince. When all other friends desert, he remains. When riches take wings and reputation falls to pieces, he is as constant in his love as the sun in its journey through the heavens. If fortune drives his master forth an outcast in the world, friendless and homeless, the faithful dog asks no higher privilege than that of accompanying him to guard against danger, to fight against his enemies. And when that last scene of all comes, and death takes his master in its embrace, and his body is laid away in the cold ground, no matter if all other friends pursue their way, there, by his graveside will the noble dog be found, his head between his paws, his eyes sad, but open in alert watchfulness, faithful and true even in death.

Mom did not have a dog to faithfully mourn her passing from this world. She just had all of us. Thank you for being here today to send her home, where I am sure she was greeted by my Grandpa Ted, and ... ALL of her dogs. Standing at the ready.

ENDNOTES

❀

1. All quotes from Kitwood, T. (1977). *Dementia reconsidered: the person comes first.* London: Open University Press, McGraw-Hill Education, McGraw-Hill House, 133, 81, 144, 119, 143.

2. U.S. Department of Health and Human Services, National Institute on Aging. (2002). *Alzheimer's disease: unraveling the mystery.* NIH Publication Number: 02-3782.

3. Reprinted with permission. Minnesota-North Dakota Chapter of the Alzheimer's Association. (2004). *www.alzmndak.org*

4. DL Bachman, PA Wolf, R Linn, JF Knoefel, J Cobb, A Belanger, RB D'Agostino and LR White. (1992). "Prevalence of dementia and probable senile dementia of the Alzheimer type in the Framingham Study," *Neurology,* 42, 115-119.

5. National Alliance for Caregiving and AARP Study. (1977).

6. Folstein, MF, Folstein SE, & McHugh, PR. (1975). "Mini-mental state: a practical method for grading the cognitive state of patients for the clinician," *Journal of Psychiatric Research,* 12, 189-198. Cockrell, JR, & Folstein, MF. (1988). "Mini-mental state examination (MMSE)," *Psychopharmacology,* 24, 689-692.

7. Alzheimer's Disease Education & Referral Center (ADEAR), a service of the National Institute on Aging. See *www.alzheimers.org/nainews*

8. The *Savvy Caregiver* material is reprinted with permission, and is copyrighted by K. Hepburn, M. Lewis, J. Tornature, & C.W. Sherman. (2001). Minneapolis, Minnesota: University of Minnesota, School of Nursing.

9. Individual approach, caregiver involvement improve quality of care and life for people with Alzheimer's disease. (2004, July 16). Philadelphia. Alzheimer's Association News Release.

10. Vest, G. (1942). Eulogy of the Dog. In Ralph L. Woods (Ed.) *A Treasury of the Familiar* (pp. 576-577). New York: Grolier, Incorporated. George G. Vest

was an attorney, and this speech is the closing argument from one of his cases in 1869. He represented a farmer whose dog, Old Drum, had been shot and killed by a neighbor. He won the case. The jury returned a verdict for the plaintiff for $500, far more than the sum sued for.

11. Mitchell, M. (2002). *Dancing on Quicksand, A Gift of Friendship in the Age of Alzheimer's* (pp. 20, 28, 31). Boulder: Johnson Books.

12. Selected resources reprinted with permission. Jack Canfield, Mark Vistor Hansen and LeAnn Thieman, L.P.N. (2004). *Chicken Soup for the Caregiver's Soul, Stories to Inspire Caregivers in the Home, the Community and the World,* (pp. 353-355), Deerfield Beach, FL, Health Communications, Inc.

ADDITIONAL RESOURCES

✽

The new culture is an invitation to us to see those whose mental powers are failing as our fellow human beings, not as strangers or aliens. We recover the sense of community, long hidden away in the depths of our collective unconscious: a place where people can accept each other with realism, and on equal terms. With this encouragement we can more easily accept the fact of our own ageing, and even the possibility that we may be among those who have dementia before we die.

TOM KITWOOD

Contact Information for the Persons and Organizations Mentioned in this Book

Colorado Chapter of the Alzheimer's Association
455 Sherman Street, Suite 500
Denver, Colorado 80203
303-813-1669, 888-535-3241
Colorado Chapter: http://www.alzrockymtn.org

The National Academy of Elder Law Attorneys, Inc. (NAELA)
1604 North Country Club Road
Tucson, Arizona 85716
520-881-4005
http://www.naela.org

Rosa Mazone
6305 West 6th Avenue, #D-19
Lakewood, Colorado 80214
303-233-5365
http://rosamazone.home.att.net

Donald Murphy, MD
Senior Care of Colorado, P.R.
1721 East 19th Avenue, Suite 574
Denver, Colorado 80218
303-869-2269

National Resources for Caregivers[12]

The ALS Association (ALSA) is a national not-for-profit voluntary health organization dedicated solely to the fight against ALS, or Amyotrophic Lateral Sclerosis (often called Lou Gehrig's disease). The mission of The ALS Association is to find a cure for and improve the lives of those living with ALS. Phone: 818-880-9007. *www.alsa.org*

The Alzheimer's Association, a national network of Chapters, is dedicated to advancing Alzheimer's research and helping those affected by the disease. The Association also provides education and support for people diagnosed with the condition, their families and caregivers. Advocacy is a major component of their mission, serving as a voice in the capitals of every state, congressional offices and the White House. Phone: 800-272-3900. *www.alz.org*

ALZwell Caregiver Support is dedicated to helping dementia caregivers to find understanding, wisdom and support throughout the caregiving journey. *www.alzwell.com*

American Association of Retired Persons (AARP) offers many free pamphlets and caregiver help. Phone: 888-687-2277. *www.aarp.org/life/caregiving*

Caregivers-USA is a free, nationwide database that puts people in touch with more than 40,000 caregiving and caregiver support services nationwide. *www.caregivers-usa.org*

Children of Aging Parents (CAPS) is a 25-year-old non-profit organization dedicated to enhancing the lives of family caregivers through information and referral services, educational outreach and the establishment and facilitation of support groups. Phone: 800-227-7294. *www.caps4caregivers.org*

Center for Advocacy for the Rights and Interests of the Elderly (CARIE) provides free telephone consultation, which includes counseling and problem resolution services to the older person, their caregivers and professionals. Phone: 215-545-5728. *www.carie.org*

The Compassionate Friends offers support groups and information for bereaved family members, and emphasizes positive resolution to grief. Phone: 708-990-0010.

Eldercare Locater is a public service, operating in conjunction with the U.S. Administration on Aging that provides referrals to local community agencies for home care, respite services, adult day care, senior centers, legal assistance, home-delivered meals and transportation. Phone: 800-677-1116. *www.eldercare.gov*

ElderCare Online provides an online community where supportive peers and professionals help caregivers improve quality of life for themselves and their aging loved ones. *www.ec-online.net*

Faith in Action, an interfaith volunteer caregiving program, invites Americans of every faith to work together to improve the lives of their neighbors of all ages with long-term health needs. There are nearly 1,000 Faith in Action programs nationwide. Phone: 877-324-8411. *www.faithinaction.org*

Family Caregiver Alliance offers programs at national, state and local levels to support and sustain caregivers. FCA is a public voice for caregivers, illuminating the daily challenges they face, offering them the assistance they need and deserve, and championing their cause through education, services, research and advocacy. Phone: 800-445-8106. *www.caregiver.org*

Leeza Gibbons Memory Foundation establishes Leeza's Places across the country for support, research, a continuum of care, political advocacy, acceptance and wellness. Leeza's Place serves as an "oasis" for education, empowerment and energy for caregivers and their recently diagnosed loved ones. Phone: 855-655-3392. *www.leezasplace.org*

Meals on Wheels of America provides hot, nourishing meals to elderly and disabled persons who are unable to provide meals for themselves. The meals, daily contact by caring volunteers, and professional case management allow frail, homebound persons to remain in their own homes ... where they want to be. Phone: 703-548-5558. *www.mowaa.org*

National Alliance for Caregiving provides support to family caregivers and the professionals who help them and increases public awareness of issues facing family caregivers. Resource guides and information are available online and in print. *www.caregiving.org*

National Council on Aging is a national network of organizations and individuals dedicated to improving the health and independence of older persons. The web site includes many publications of interest to caregivers. Phone: 800-373-4906. *www.ncoa.org*

National Family Caregivers Association (NFCA) is the only constituency organization that reaches across the boundaries of different diagnoses, different relationships and different life stages to address the common needs and concerns of all family caregivers. Phone: 800-896-3650. *www.thefamilycaregiver.org*

National Hospice & Palliative Care Organization (NHPCO) is committed to improving end-of-life care and expanding access to hospice care with the goal of enhancing quality of life for people living with a life-limiting illness and their loved ones. NHPCO can provide information on hospice and help people locate a hospice or palliative care provider in their area. Phone: 800-658-8898. *www.hospiceinfo.org*

Rosalynn Carter Institute for Caregiving promotes the mental health and well-being of individuals, families, and professional caregivers through research, education and training. Its focus is on generic caregiving that pertains to all caregivers across various illnesses and disabilities; incorporation of both lay and professional points of view; and collaboration among front-line caregivers, academicians and students to improve the caregiving process. Phone: 912-928-1234. *www.RosalynnCarter.org*

Today's Caregiver magazine includes up-to-the-minute advice on topics such as incontinence, grandparent caregiving, mobility, Alzheimer's, cancer and ALS caregiving, as well as interviews with celebrity caregivers. The magazine produces *The Fearless Caregiver* book and conferences and hosts an online caregiver community. Phone: 800-829-2734. *www.caregiver.com*

Well Spouse Foundation is an association of spousal caregivers who form friendships with other caregivers in similar situations. Phone: 800-838-0879. *www.wellspouse.org*

RECOMMENDATIONS
FOR FURTHER READING

❀

A Dignified Life: The Best Friends Approach to Alzheimer's Care, A Guide for Family Caregivers, Virginia Bell, M.S.W. & David Troxel, M.P.H., Deerfield Beach, FL, Health Communications, Inc. (2002).

Chicken Soup for the Caregiver's Soul, Stories to Inspire Caregivers in the Home, the Community and the World, Jack Canfield, Mark Vistor Hansen and LeAnn Thieman, L.P.N., Deerfield Beach, FL, Health Communications, Inc. (2004).

Cutting Loose: An Adult's Guide to Coming to Terms With Your Parents, Howard M. Halpern, Ph.D., Simon & Schuster, New York (1976).

You Can Heal Your Life, Louise L. Hay, Carlsbad, CA, Hay House, Inc. (1984).

Alzheimer's A to Z, Secrets to Successful Caregiving, Jytte Lokvig, BA, MA, Santa Fe, NM, Endless Circle Press (2002).

The 36-Hour Day, A Family Guide to Caring for Persons with Alzheimer Disease, Related Dementing Illnesses, and Memory Loss in Later Life, Nancy L. Mace, M.A. and Peter V. Rabins, M.D., M.P.H., New York, NY, Warner Books (2001).

Dancing on Quicksand, A Gift of Friendship in the Age of Alzheimer's, Marilyn Mitchell, Boulder, CO, Johnson Publishing (2002).

Coping with Alzheimer's: A Caregiver's Emotional Survival Guide, Rose Oliver, Ph.D. and Frances A. Bock, Ph.D, North Hollywood, CA, Melium Powers Wilshire Book Company (1987).

How Did I Become My Parent's Parent?, Harriet Sarnoff Schiff, New York, NY, Viking Penguin, a division of Penguin Books (1996).

❀

Share your
path to peace
through Alzheimer's
with us at:

www.SteppingStonesToPeace.com

❀

INDEX

❀

Advance directives, 43-45
  Defined, 43
  Types of, 44-45
    General durable power of
      attorney, 44-45
    Living will, 44
    Medical durable power of
      attorney, 44
Agent, 43-45
Alzheimer's Association, 57-68
  How to locate your local
    Chapter, 26, 157-159
  How they can help you, 23, 26
  Newsletter, 26, 68
  Referral lists, 26, 34, 55, 66,
    68, 100
  Savvy Caregiver Program,
    58-65
  Support groups, 59, 66, 110,
    126
Alzheimer's-type dementia
  Definition, 10
  Diagnosis, 27-35
    Early diagnosis, benefits of,
      16, 31-32
    First step on your path to
      peace, 16, 19
    Folstein Mini Mental State
      Examination, 28-29
    How obtained
      Autopsy, 30
      PET scan, 30

Alzheimer's-type dementia.
    (*continued*)
    How obtained (*continued*)
      Medical history, 30
    How a diagnosis can help
      you, 16-17, 31-32
    MMSE, 28-29, 33
    Personal history, 30, 34
    Role of geriatrician, 22, 32
  Stages (symptoms), 11-13
    Early (mild), 11
    Middle (moderate), 12
    Late (severe), 13
    Mental declines, 11-13, 58-63
      Memory, 59
      Language, 60
      Reasoning, 61
      Paranoia and suspicion, 62
      Problem solving, 62-63
    Physical declines, 11-13, 63-65
      Gait and balance, 63
      Incontinence, 63
      Personal hygiene, 64
Attorney. *See* Elder Law attorney

Being vs. Doing. *See* Roles

Caregiver roles
  Advocate for loved one, 38, 41,
    54, 86, 94, 144, 147
  Advocate with professionals, 41,
    54

Caregiver roles (*continued*)
　Companion, 72, 93-100, 130,
　　144-145
Childhood Box, x, 5, 98, 104-105,
　　107-109, 111, 113, 115,
　　119, 122-124, 129, 144,
　　147-148
　Identifying contents, x, 98, 114,
　　117, 119-120, 129
　Healing childhood wounds, x,
　　71, 77-78, 80, 97, 105,
　　114, 118, 123, 129, 145
　Releasing the past, 101-110
　Loved-one's box, 104-105, 107,
　　110, 115, 122, 146
Connecting with your loved one
　Ability to perform tasks, 64
　Communication tips, 139
　Emotional support through
　　compassionate listening,
　　4, 128
　Focusing on remaining abilities,
　　95-96, 100, 124
　Learning life stories, 115
　Nonverbal communication, 121
Conservatorship, 41, 62

Declaration as to medical or
　　surgical treatment. *See*
　　Living will
Dementia
　Causes, 22, 26, 30
　Facts about, 58-59
　See also Alzheimer's-type
　　dementia
Diagnosis. *See* Alzheimer's-type
　dementia
Dictionary of life. *See* Thinking
　strategies

Doctor Visits
　Evaluation for Alzheimer's,
　　28-29
　Tips for visit, 19, 34-35
Doing vs. Being. *See* Roles
Driving
　Tips for stopping, 61
Durable Power of Attorney. *See*
　　Advance directives

Education about Alzheimer's
　Alzheimer's Association, 57-68
　Helps you to
　　Expect the unexpected, 31,
　　　58, 65, 81
　　Adjust your expectations, 31,
　　　66-67, 75, 81, 120, 123,
　　　137
　　Structure time with your
　　　loved one, 85-91
　　Develop appropriate
　　　supports, 21-26, 31,
　　　59-64, 81, 115
　　Neutralize negative
　　　emotions, 33, 65, 68,
　　　75-81, 83-84, 138
　　Mental and physical declines,
　　　11-13, 59-65
　Stages of Alzheimer's, 11-13
Elder Law attorney
　Defined, 42
　Scope of practice, 23, 42-45
　How an Elder Law attorney can
　　help you, 23, 42-45
　Legal capacity, 41
　Tips for locating, 50-53
　　National Academy of Elder
　　　Law Attorneys, 51, 158
　　Meeting questions, 52

Elder Law attorney (*continued*)
Tips for locating (*continued*)
Screening questions, 51-52
Referrals, 50
Fee arrangements, 52-53
Financial Planning Checklist,
46-47

Financial planning, 45-50
How financial planning can
help you, 45-50
Members of your financial
planning team, 46
Financial Planning Checklist,
46-47
Financial power of attorney. *See*
Advance directives
Folstein Mini Mental State
Examination (MMSE),
28-29, 33
Contents, 28-29
Scoring, 28

General durable power of
attorney. *See* Advance
directives
Geriatrician
Definition, 22
How to locate a local
geriatrician, 26, 34
How a geriatrician can help
you, 22, 27-32
Gifts of dementia, 143-150
Loving myself, 144-145
Loving my mother, 146-147
Third step on your path to
peace, 4, 82
Transforming my relationship
with my family, 147
Guardianship, 41, 62

Hard-wiring, 5, 86, 96, 102, 104,
109, 113, 133
How dementia changed my
mother, 101-105
Changes in job description,
103-104
Changes in personality, 104
Mother's box, 104-105, 107,
110, 115, 122, 146
Growing up childlike views, x,
71, 77-78, 80, 97, 105,
114, 118, 123, 129, 145
Health care power of attorney. *See*
Advance directives

Living Will. *See* Advance directives
Long-term care, paying for, 48-50
Medicare, 48
Medicaid, 49-50
Long-term care insurance, 50
How to choose insurance, 49

Medicaid, 49-50
Medical durable power of
attorney. *See* Advance
directives
Medicare, 48
MMSE. *See* Folstein Mini Mental
State Examination

Power of attorney. *See* Advance
directives
Principal, 43-45

Questions, 4
How can I stay open to the gifts
this experience has to
offer?, 85-91
Leave your own agenda at
home, 93-100

Questions (*continued*)
  How can I stay open to the gifts
       this experience has to
       offer? (*continued*)
     Let go of the past, 101-110
     Reveal your true self, 111-118
     Pay attention to your loved
       one as if she is a
       prophet, 119-126
  How do I prepare myself for
       this journey?, 69-84
     Make an inventory of your
       thoughts, 74-77
     Practice better thinking,
       77-80
     Learn as much as you can
       about dementia, 80-81
  Who can I turn to for
       information and
       support?, 21-26
     Geriatrician, 27-34
     Elder Law attorney, 37-55
     Alzheimer's Association,
       57-68
Quotes
  Baker, Ivy, 27
  Bard, Carl, 57
  Carter, Rosalynn, 143
  de Saint-Exupery, Antoine, 133
  Einstein, Albert, 151
  Ellis, Mary Relindes, v
  Hahn, Thich Nhat, 101
  Havel, Vaclav, 1
  Horace, 37
  Kitwood, Tom, 4, 76, 86, 94, 157
  L'Amour, Louis, 93
  Lao-Tzu, 9, 85
  Lokvig, Jytte, 121
  Mitchell, Marilyn, 139
  O'Connor, Sandra Day, 21

Quotes (*continued*)
  Proust, Marcel, 127
  Reagan, Ronald, 69
  Vest, George G., 153
  Wilder, Laura Ingalls, 119
  Williams, Tennessee, 111

Roles
  Doing vs. being, 93-100
  Inventory, 74-75, 94-98
  Identifying lifelong patterns, 78,
       107-108, 114, 129-130,
       138
  Reversals, 95, 107, 135

Statistics
  Causes of dementia, 22
  Changes in the brain, plaques
       and tangles, 10
  Cost of Alzheimer's care to
       society, 45
  Cost of care in a nursing home,
       23, 49
  Who are caregivers, 24
  Home care, 85
  Life expectancy with, 3, 45
  Number of American families
       affected by, 3, 85
  Number of American's afflicted,
       45, 85
Stories
  Getting Mom to the doctor,
       14-16
  Brushing her teeth, 57-58
  Tennis shoes, 63
  We love each other a lot,
       102-103
  Her eyes said it all, 120-122
  Washing her hair, 105-106
  Hansel & Gretel, 111-113

Stories (*continued*)
    Reading, 134-137

Thinking strategies, 69-84
    Dictionary of life, 73, 79, 94, 99,
        107-108, 128, 131, 144
    Thinking makes it so, 72
    Inventory of thoughts, 74-75
    Sources of thoughts, 75-77
    Changing negative
        interpretations, 77-78
    Second step on your path to
        peace, 4, 72

Thinking strategies (*continued*)
    Suggestions for practicing new
        thoughts, 78-80
    Supporting new thoughts with
        knowledge, 80-81
Time commitment, 85-91
    Regular schedule, 87-88
    How to structure, 85-91
    Meditation for staying focused,
        88, 93-126

ORDER FORM

Mom, Are You There?
Finding a Path to Peace through Alzheimer's
KATHLEEN A. NEGRI

FAX ORDERS: 303-393-7398. Complete and send this form.

WEB ORDERS: www.SteppingStonesToPeace.com

POSTAL ORDERS: forget-me-not press, P.O. Box 587,
Wheat Ridge, Colorado 80034-0587

Please send me ____ copies at $17.00 each
(price subject to change) . . . . $_____

SALES TAX: Please add 7.2 % for products shipped to
Colorado addresses (tax subject to change). . . . . . . $_____

SHIPPING: U.S.: $4.00 for first book;
$2.00 for each additional book
INTERNATIONAL: $9.00 for first book;
$5.00 for each additional book . . . . $_____

TOTAL . . . . $_____

PAYMENT:
☐ CHECK or MONEY ORDER enclosed, payable to forget-me-not press
☐ CREDIT CARD

☐ Mastercard   ☐ VISA   ☐ Discover   ☐ AMEX

Card No.: _____

Exp. Date: _____

Signature: _____

Name on Card: _____

Street Address: _____

City/State/ZIP: _____

Daytime Phone: _____

E-mail Address: _____